Boccaccio in Florence

Also by W.D. Jackson

Then and Now:

Then and Now — Words in the Dark (Menard Press)
From Now to Then (Menard Press)

W.D. Jackson

Boccaccio in Florence
and other poems

From *Then and Now — Opus 3*

Shearsman Books
Exeter

First published in the United Kingdom in 2009 by
Shearsman Books Ltd
58 Velwell Road
Exeter EX4 4LD

and

The Menard Press
8 The Oaks
Woodside Avenue
London N12 8AR

www.shearsman.com

ISBN   978-1-84861-068-2
First edition

Copyright © W.D. Jackson, 2009
All rights reserved.

Acknowledgements
The translations/versions of poems by Ernst Jandl in this volume are based on poems from the following volumes: *Laut und Luise* (1966); *Der künstliche Baum* (1970, *der gelbe hund* (1980), *sprechblasen. verstreute gedichte 3* (1997); *dingfest. verstreute gedichte 4* (1997). The last two books are part of the 10-volume collected edition, *Poetische Werk* (1997); the poems from the first three volumes have since been republished in that same edition; all are copyright © Luchterhand Literaturverlag, 1997.
The versions offered here are published by kind permission of Luchterhand Literaturverlag, Munich.

Cover image:
Paula Rego: 'The Cake Woman', 2004 (private collection).
Pastel on paper, mounted on aluminium,150 x 150 cm.
Image courtesy of Marlborough Fine Art, London.
Copyright © Paula Rego, 2004.
Reproduced by permission of the artist.

Contents

The Dance of Death	9
From Boccaccio in Florence	
i The Dream	29
ii The Convent Garden	36
iii Nastagio degli Onesti and the Necromancer	42
The Chest	51
The Gift	67
Rainer Maria Rilke: A Post-Romantic Portrait (On Poetry and Death)	71
after jandl	99
From Self-Portrait as a White-Collar Worker (4)	
i Working for the Enemy	118
ii North of the Future	
—The Curse	120
—An Ordinary Day	120
—The Blessing	122
Acknowledgements & Notes	124

BOCCACCIO IN FLORENCE
& OTHER POEMS

THE DANCE OF DEATH
(after *Todtentanz der Stadt Basel*)

"Dance, dance, dance till you drop"
    W.H. Auden, *Death's Echo*

i

The Pope

Come, Holy Father, show them how
You do the dance and make your bow.
Though triple-crowned and double-crossed,
Your powers to bind and loose are lost.

*

Alive, they called me 'Your Holiness'.
Selling indulgences made me wealthy.
I was God's mouth on earth, no less—
But now my breath couldn't smell less healthy.

ii

The Emperor

Imperial Highness, grim and grey,
It's too late now for looking sorry:
I'll pipe you down death's dusty way.
So off you dance—I'm in a hurry.

*

Able not only to defend
My empire but to make it bigger,
Here I cut a sorry figure:
Death's dominion has no end.

iii

The Empress

Empress, for you I'll demonstrate
The dance—just trip along behind.
The court has left you to your fate.
Dance, dance while I rob you blind.

*

A lusty life I thought I led
As a rich kaiser's fubsy *Frau*.
I've danced my last dance, anyhow,
And lack all pride and joy, being dead—

iv

The King

O King, relax. Don't waste your breath
On giving orders. My thin hand
Makes all men weak and powerless, and
Crowns their bowed heads with a dry wreath.

*

Living, I loved to wield my power,
Raised to the highest ranks of honour.
And now? I'm nothing but a goner:
Shackled and gagged, I await my hour.

v

The Queen

Queenie, your fun and games are over,
So down you flop into your grave.
Your beauty, health and wealth can't save
Your face—from pushing up the clover.

*

Oh help, where are my maids to cheer
And grace my chamber? Someone please
Come here and set my mind at ease!
Or is my end so near? . . .

vi

The Cardinal

Off you waltz in your crimson hat,
Monseigneur, mind you don't fall flat!
You've blessed or cursed the dead with a text,
But I'm afraid it's your turn next.

*

I was a well-known Cardinal,
An apple of the papal eye:
The whole world honoured me—must I
Keep dancing till I fall?

vii

The Bishop

Learned defender of the Faith,
Bishop, you've often turned aside
Into the primrose way of pride.
But you can't run away from death.

*

Flattered by sacristan and flunkey
As long as I lived as a Reverend Sir,
Breathing death's deconstructed air
I dance and chatter like a monkey.

viii

The Duke

With ladies you have danced, proud Duke,
And had them come and had them go.
The dead may make you want to puke,
But take their hands and say hello.

*

Dammit, must I be off so quickly
And leave land, friends, wife, children, fame
Behind, until I look the same
As these—as thin and sickly?

ix

The Duchess

*My gracious lady, be of good cheer!
Although you come of a noble line,
Loved and respected by all up here,
Down there, my love, you're mine all mine.*

*

My lute is cracked. And no dissembling
Affects this bony dancing horror.
Duchess today but not tomorrow,
I dance in fear and trembling.

x

The Earl

*Although my news has brought no joy,
My lord, feed* me *in your French cuisine,
Before you hop it . . . Or are you* itching
To join the hoi polloi?

*

A noble earl I was. My name
Was known and feared in all the world,
But death has danced me off and hurled
Me down, and felled my fame.

xi

The Abbot

Abbot, come here and let me knock
Your mitre off and break your staff.
Good shepherds always put their flock
First. You're good for a laugh.

*

I rose to be abbot, biggest of brothers,
And lived empowered and honoured, until
Nobody dared oppose my will.
But death has culled me like the others.

xii

The Knight

Sir Knight, your name is on my list.
Your sword-hand had the power to kill,
But the thrust of my armour-piercing fist
Cannot be parried by strength or skill.

*

A conscientious, valiant knight,
I served the world with derring-do.
Breaking my order's rules, I now
Must dance a last good-night.

xiii

The Lawyer

No dodge or obsequious flattery
Can get you off; there's no appeal.
My prison cells set no one free,
Cleric or lay. I over-rule.

*

Man's law derives from God on high,
As all may read in learned books.
Lawyers should not behave like crooks,
But love the truth and hate to lie.

xiv

The Alderman

Although a gent of this great city,
One who's done business here, and sat
On board and council and committee,
Please bow your head while I eat your hat.

*

I worked my fingers to the bone
To see the common good protected.
Both rich and poor should be respected,
Not live or die as if on their own.

xv

The Canon

O Canon, chanting loud and clear,
Leading your nice cathedral choir,
Listen: my scrannel pipe shrieks higher.
—Life's old sweet song croaks here.

*

I loved to swank in cope and frock,
And warble sacred melodies:
Death's clashing discords cut through these
And gave me a nasty shock.

xvi

The Doctor

Doctor, please check my anatomy,
That all is as it ought to be.
You used to treat, for a fat fee,
Patients who shortly looked like me!

*

An expert in urology,
I hoped to help both man and wife.
Who'll check *my* water, now that my life
Is pissing away so rapidly?

xvii

The Nobleman

Come, noble warrior, sheathe your sword,
And screw, if you want to save your face,
Your courage to the sticking place.
Death is the hero's last reward.

*

I terrified my enemies,
Though armed and in harness cap-à-pie—
As death has seized and rattled *me,*
Grimly forcing me to my knees.

xviii

The Lady

Milady, all this beauty-care
Is nothing but a purblind error.
Your body—skin—face—hair—
Are grey as ashes. Look in your mirror.

*

My eyes were blue, my hair was gold,
But all I can see in my mirror's a skull.
What a horrible shock! What a drag! How dull
To feel my blood run cold.

xix

The Merchant

*Business as usual, sir? Well, not
Much longer. Though a proper toff,
Nothing you've got can buy me off.
Come dance till you rot.*

*

My time was money, and I learned
To get rich quick by ruthless thrift.
But death, devaluing my gift,
Robs me of everything I earned.

xx

The Abbess

*My lady Abbess, full of grace,
How flat your little tummy's grown.
But I've no need to cast a stone!
Or cut off my nose to spite my face.*

*

I've read my Bible, sung from the Psalter—
No hymn or prayer can help me now
To put off when or impede how
Death leads me to the altar.

xxi

The Cripple

Hobbledehoy on your ancient crutch,
I'll help you limp, I'll help you hop.
You may not count for very much,
But come and dance with me till you drop.

*

Dragging along as if in fetters,
I'm neither use nor ornament.
With death as my friend I'm more than content
To dance and hobnob with my betters.

xxii

The Hermit

Brother, stop cowering in your cell.
Come out, stand still, while I douse your light.
With your long white beard, you know very well
You've a journey to undertake tonight.

*

Sackcloth and ashes I have worn,
Which hasn't done my health much good.
No longer safe in my cell in the wood,
Was it for this that I was born?

xxiii

The Youth

*Where are you off to now, my lad?
I'll show you a path which leads elsewhere,
To a private place. Though I'm afraid
Lots of laddish lovers lie there.*

*

Wining and dining and having it off in
Bordellos run by fat madames,
My life was nothing but fun and games . . .
I never dreamt I'd fill a coffin . . .

xxiv

The Usurer

*Your money's of no use to me,
You crooked, god-forsaken Croesus.
Your tables were overturned by Jesus.
Now I'm your private company.*

*

I set no store by Jesus Christ:
Business pre-occupied my mind.
But all my savings stay behind—
Where life is prized, not priced.

xxv

The Young Woman

My dear, your lovely rose-red mouth
Will soon be pale. No boring wife,
With boys you've danced away your youth:
With me you'll dance away your life.

*

Help, help! Though I don't want to die,
Life's somehow not much fun any more.
Even the Dance of Death's a bore,
Forget it. And so, *Goodbye, goodbye* . . .

xxvi

The Piper

What reel will you play on your bagpipes now?
'The Beggar Boy' or 'Black Man's Jig'?
No fair was fun without you. How
Can you not join my whirligig?

*

That's it then. Before I ran out of luck
No fair was too far for me to travel.
My piper's motley sleeves unravel.
I lost my pipes while drunk.

xxvii

The Herald

Herald! your red official hat
No longer serves to distinguish you.
Nor does your mace, or drum's rat-a-tat.
Shut up while I extinguish you!

*

Emperor and princes knew my worth:
My purse was heavy, stables stocked.
Many who heard my voice were shocked,
But death has filled my mouth with earth.

xxviii

The Mayor

Now, Mr Mayor, you know it's time
For body and soul to call it a day.
Playing my lute, I sing and rhyme:
Come dance while I rhyme and sing and play.

*

I tried in my judicial role
To see that fair was fair, not fudged.
On the day that rich and poor are judged,
May God have mercy on my soul.

xxix

The Executioner

*Disposer of other people's lives,
In your red jerkin and fur hat,
You don't look happy. But so what?
After I've sentenced them, no one survives.*

*

As all who dared to look could see,
I treated everyone alike:
A faithful servant of the Reich,
I discharged my duties peacefully.

xxx

The Fool

*Hey-diddle-diddle, come dance to my fiddle,
And jump with me over the moon.
Poor fool, leave your bauble, don't dally or dawdle.
Are you cold? You'll be colder soon.*

*

I'd sooner be beaten black and yellow
Four times a day by my lord and his thugs—
Lug logs home—live off bugs or slugs—
Than fight with this bony fellow!

xxxi

The Pedlar

You, penny-pinching pedlar, come—
You petty swindler and crier-up-allies—
And let some shameless factotum
Flog your knicknacks to bimboes and wallies.

*

I've travelled far by river and road,
Exchanging foreign currencies:
Dollars, crowns, guilders, gold guineas.—
Who'll pay me now what I'm owed?

xxxii

The Blindman

Ragged old blindman, no one can save
Your bacon. In your hour of need,
Allow me to cut your guide-dog's lead
And show you to your grave.

*

I can't earn my keep or my daily bread.
As blind as a lemon or a log,
I can't go a step without my dog.
Thank God I'll soon be dead.

xxxiii

The Cook

John Cook, roll over here. You've got
So fat that you can hardly trot.
You love sweet puddings. But the hour
Has struck which turns all stomachs sour.

*

I've basted capons, roasted geese,
Steamed fish for king and nobleman.
Venison, pâté, marzipan—
My belly aches to leave all these.

xxxiv

The Peasant

You've laboured long in the sweat of your brow,
From dawn to dusk, each day without fail.
I'll free you from your burdens now:
Hand me your basket—dagger—and flail.

*

Hey, give me back my old felt hat!
I don't mind working any more,
As I've always worked. I'm old and poor
And weary. But what's wrong with that?

xxxv

The Poet

Poet, put down your raging pen:
Your artful words won't help you when
I come for you like other men
(Death's 'now' has neither 'then' nor 'then') . . .

You've given me shocking / mocking lines.
Are you (or your family) better prepared
Than the Pope et al., to whom you've dared
Assign such cries and groans? . . .

And who on earth is ever ready
To greet me with a cool and steady
Look? Death's nothing but what you make it.
The choice is yours. You can take / not take it.

*

. . .

xxxvi

The Poet's Wife

Mother and wife, you needn't grieve
For them much longer. Depend upon it,

The time is ripe for you to leave.
Let me relieve you of your bonnet.

*

I've always been resigned to death,
Always believed in eternal life;
But this hard double-grief, as wife
And mother, sorely tests my faith.

Coda

Adam and Eve

"... *how you take it!*" —The Tempest

If she and I had ever been
At home in Eden, original sin
Entered our minds when we questioned why
We of all creatures had to die.

Made in God's image, or so we thought,
Our SELF-IMPORTANCE filled the air,
Oceans and all the earth . . . , till nowhere
Was safe from the fire with which we fought . . .

Stealer of fire, and then fire's slave,
Afraid of what we'll lose or find
Today—tomorrow—or in the grave—
The what-if / what-if-nots of the mind—

Our self-assertive song and dance
Contrives to shift the blame

To God or Life-and-Death or Chance.—
Victims in all but name,

Our world is, still, the way we make it:
Death's a blank fact like other facts
Of life. And life is—how you take it.
I *think*, therefore I *act*.

For man alone, of all that dies
Passively under the passive sun,
Is blessed with active words and eyes
To do / undo what's done / undone.

*

"*Rose, oh reiner Widerspruch, Lust,
Niemandes Schlaf zu sein unter soviel
Lidern.*"

Thus Rilke wrote—for his own or any
Gravestone—consumed by pain like fire:
"Rose, oh pure contradiction, desire
To be no one's sleep under so many
Eyelids."

(2006)

From **BOCCACCIO IN FLORENCE:**
  Three Stories and a Dream

"Al quale ella, quasi ridendo disse:
'Buon uomo, el mi par che tu sogni.'"
                    Decameron II,v

   i

   The Dream

May, 1348. The sun was sinking
Behind the campanile. Boccaccio knelt
Inside the still unfinished duomo, thinking
Of what he'd seen, and wondering how he felt
About the immortal Architect . . . Could He
Have *planned* this plague, this 'Great Mortality'?

Whole houses, great palazzi, emptied of
Their occupants, the dead piled up outside
With oozing tumours. Rat-packs freely roved
Deserted streets, where pigs and dogs had died
From mauling corpses or infected rags,
And looters staggered under bursting bags.

Abandoned children cried. The sick were left
To die alone, their bodies left to rot.
The stench of dead or dying people bereft
Him of all words. But some he knew were not
So easily shocked. All forms of strange excess
Flourished—helped stave off horror and distress.

Men dropped down dead in the street by day and night.
Coffins and grave-plots were a rarity.
Rough gangs of paupers dug deep plague-pits right

Across old churchyards, charging a fat fee
To stow the dead in tiers with a thin layer
Of soil between. And more for a priest or a prayer.

But most were thrown in like dead goats or sheep . . .
Which stopped him trying to pray. Instead, he sat
And closed his aching eyes, and fell asleep,
And dreamt he'd travelled home to Naples—at
The market, where he'd come to buy a horse.
But all the horses were half-dead, or worse.

And all their grooms and riders were half-dead
And putrefying slowly. Stinking meat,
Alive with maggots, and the grinning head
Of a huge boar, were all there was to eat.
One stall had bursting figs, egg-plants, milk, honey,
But no one left alive to take his money.

And so he waved his bulging bag of gold
To bring them back to life: five hundred florins.
A pretty girl strolled past. From how she strolled
He knew she'd like to go with him to Florence.
She smiled and said she was his bastard sister.
I'm illegitimate too, he cried, and kissed her.

Safe in her rooms, she wore a veil-like dress
With living leaves and slowly opening flowers
Which he could see straight through. In less
Than no time he'd been there for hours and hours.
Her black eyes flashed. Fresh fruit and roasted meat
And wine appeared. OK, she laughed, let's eat.

And so they ate, drank, laughed, till very late.
As children we'd have shared a double bed,
She coyly giggled. Let's not curse our fate

But make up for it now. He gawped. She said,
Although we had one dad, a different womb
Had *us* . . . Or would you like a separate room?

My sweet, she whispered, now I've got you here
Locked in my soft white arms, within their pale,
I'll be a park and you can be my deer,
Feed where you want to feed, up hill down dale,
Graze on my lips, or if their slopes are dry
Look lower, where my rough moist-pastures lie.

At this he smiled and, since the night was hot,
They took each other's clothes off, kissed and groped,
And tried it standing up before they got
Into her bed. But, as she must have hoped,
He wanted to relieve himself before
Proceeding. Over there, she said. That door.

And off he dashed. Outside a loosened plank
Shot up and he shot down into the filth
Of many years. The next house was a bank,
In which his father sat, while his own wealth
Was counted by the old man's bastard daughter.
He closed his eyes. A stream of lukewarm water

Splashed off his chest. Shrieking with laughter, high
On the one remaining plank spanning the alley,
She squatted till she'd finished. That pig-sty
's the perfect place for you, she whooped. You wally!
He scraped away both fresh and ancient dirt.
No broken bones. But now his pride was hurt.

And, leaping the six-foot wall which separated
Sump from side-road, he found his sister's door—
Where he yelled and banged in vain. Infuriated,

And feeling very nude, he banged and swore
At the blank windows. Till her sleepy bully
Opened one, dropped his clothes out, and said dully

Wake me again, friend, and I'll knock you cold.
The thick black beard and scars of this tough guy
Convinced his doxy's brother that the gold
Was gone for good. He raged. But, rather than die
On his sister's door-step, donned his shoes and shirt
And stumped off down the road, stinking of dirt.

But which, and where, was his inn? Beside the sea?
This was no town for wandering round at night.
Two hulks approached. Cut-throats perhaps. So he,
Exposed and helpless, side-stepped out of sight
Into a hut. But in they stepped as well.
By Christ, they huffed and phewed, what's that foul smell?

Holding his nose, one raised their dingy lamp,
Which lit up B., who, trapped and trembling, told
His tale of woe, inspiring them to thump
His dirt-caked back. You'd have lost more than gold,
They sniggered, if you'd dozed off in that bed.
Now come and help us crack a tomb instead.

The archbishop's dead, and buried in full regalia.
His ruby ring alone is worth five hundred
Florentine florins. B. noted, *inter alia*,
This ring could save his face, and also wondered
How much the bishop's vestments might be worth,
And all the other stuff he'd left on earth.

The only problem is, they groaned, you smell
Worse than a cess-pit, or like putrid flesh.
But halfway to the duomo there's a well

We'll let you down in. Then, if you smell fresh
Enough for church, we'll show you how to rob
Its rich to feed the poor. A damned good job!

So at the well they made him mount the bucket,
And wound him down until he hit the water.
Just then—a piece of filthy rotten luck—it
Chanced that the watch, checking that run-down quarter,
Felt like a drink. The fly-by-nights did a flit,
Leaving their new friend stuck once more in the shit.

As he knew, and didn't know. Once down he drank
His fill before performing his ablutions.
Up went the bucket. But the water stank.
The watch suspected poison or pollution:
Perhaps a murdered corpse. Then B.'s wet head
Popped over the rim of the well. They howled and fled.

B. scanned their lethal weapons. Could his inn
Be somehow *in* the duomo? His two friends
Smiled yes it could—began, then, breaking in
To where the bishop lay. To make amends
For running off, they grinned, they'd let poor B.
Enter the grave and say what he could see.

The vault had one immensely heavy lid
Of marble. Flights of stone-cold marble stairs
Faded to where a foetid darkness hid
The archbishop and the bones of his forebears.
B. reeled, and retched in horror. But they said,
You go in there alive, or go in dead.

Shaking with fear, B. squeezed into the hole
They'd levered open. First he stole the ring
And hid it in his pocket. Then he stole

The bishop's crozier, mitre, everything
Worth snitching he could strip or cut from the body.
Naked, Monsignor looked a proper noddy.

—But where's the ring? the furious bully-boys
Hissed down. It must be somewhere. Look again!
B. looked, until an unexpected noise
Of footsteps made the burglars change their plan.
Grabbing their swag, they scarpered quickly. But
First they dislodged their jemmies. The lid slammed shut.

B. couldn't budge it. Overcome with fear,
He fainted by the faintly glowing stiff.
Recovered, he was sure he'd starve in there
Or go stark staring mad. And even if
They disinterred him, he'd still come to grief.
The grave was robbed, and he'd be hanged as a thief.

Or could it be he was already dead?
The air was blacker than the blackest ink,
Drowning all words and blotting out B's head.
He cried out loud. His cry and the stifling stink
Of dusty death must mean he hadn't died—
As must the night-watch, now arrived outside . . .

And then, within his dream, in some strange way
B. realized he was dreaming—only dreaming.
Which means that I don't really have to stay
In here, he thought. In fact, I'll try re-dreaming
Those voices into—what? Another gang?
I'm not dead yet. Death's sickle can go hang.

And so the gang heaved up the heavy lid,
But no big bravo wanted to go in.
A priest among them sneered and sleekly slid

His legs through, jumping out of his snake's skin
When B. grabbed hold of them, and started to haul
Him down into the grave—legs, arse and all.

The priest began to kick and then to yell.
B. held on tight. The gangsters howled and fled.
Like a black flapping crow released from hell,
The priest fled too. Thus, very far from dead,
With the ring now on his finger, self-endowed
With life and luck, Boccaccio laughed out loud

And woke. Before him in the thickening dark
A group of girls were laughing with three men
About another girl called *Alibech*.
Boccaccio counted altogether ten,
As *Filostrato* begged *Fiammetta's* pardon
For telling one about a convent garden . . .

Boccaccio listened—couldn't help but smile . . .
Nastagio degli Onesti's heartless way
With women next beguiled them for a while.
Outside the plague still raged. Ten people. Say
Each told ten stories. Three plus one makes four,
To start with. Which makes ninety-six tales more . . .

ii

The Convent Garden

Not far from Florence lies a convent, whose
Nuns are devout, whose panoramic views
Are justly famous—but which we won't name,
For fear of spoiling so much well-earned fame . . .
Its ancient gardener, Nuto, who had come
From elsewhere, now felt ripe for going home
To doze beneath his neighbours' apple-trees
In gardens where no jumpy nuns could tease
Or tell him off or giggle and hide his tools.
—"They'd blare like ewes on heat. A flock of fools!"
He'd crudely croak, once home, to anyone
Who'd listen: "Never cross a rutting nun."
Then Nuto died. His neighbour was a young
Mild-mannered man whose older wife's sharp tongue
Was often heard excoriating him.
Masetto was his name—tall, strong, and slim
About the hips and buttocks. When they buried
Old Nuto, young Masetto had been married
For just two years. Two years which seemed two lives.
He stared at all the wrinkled, withered wives
Whose men were mouldering corpses. A last few
Were staggering under the bier. "There's nothing new,"
Masetto thought, "in heaven or earth. What fun
It must be, though, to do it with a nun!"
But now the dead man's brothers were in tears:
"A few more years they have, just a few years.
One woman brought them in. Another woman
Will see them out. Poor Nuto's case is common.
But not for me, no thank you, not just yet!
At break of day tomorrow, off I set.—
For though it's been no more than two short years,

God knows I've wept tin buckets full of tears
Since feeding at the trough of married life.
Some praise its pleasures, but my loud-mouthed wife
Has caused me nothing but expense and trouble.
Conjugal bliss? I've pricked that bitter bubble!
And yet, God also knows, the neighbours say—
Particularly the women, by the way—
My wife is true and steadfast, the best kind
Of cheerful helpmate you could hope to find.
But he who wears the shoe knows where it pinches.
At first she praised me for my extra inches:
Too big for her I was, or so she claimed—
And humped me like a rabbit. Till, well-tamed,
I married her. But, only shortly after,
I was the butt of her and her friends' laughter.
The rows we've had! It does no good to curse her.
I'll knock her flat one day. Or vice versa.
She thought I was a big, soft, harmless brute.
High time I went! She'll like the extra loot.
When I first saw her hard face at our fair,
I thought she was a thief, if not a whore;
And though she's made me want her, if the truth
Were told about my wife, I'd say she's both."

Next evening, at the convent's kitchen door,
Masetto stood pretending to be poor
And begged with hand-signs, as if born deaf-mute.
The convent being a house of good repute,
This subterfuge, he hoped, would get him in
By prompting thoughts of virtue, not of sin.
The steward eyed his rags and read his signs,
But not his mind, and thought, "Before he dines,
I'll give this strong young lout those logs to chop
Which Nuto couldn't." Masetto chopped non-stop,
Hoicking huge bundles on his powerful back

And storing the wood in one long tidy stack
Against the kitchen wall beneath the eaves.
"There's more that he could do before he leaves,"
The steward urged the abbess. "Let him stay
For now," she trilled, "and get stuck in. In May
Hedges, weeds, lawns, need seeing to twice a week.
A deaf-mute shouldn't give the girls much cheek!
Be sure he gets a decent pair of pants."
Masetto eavesdropped, rubbing his red hands,
And laughed: "Your flowers and bushes shall be more
Thoroughly seen to now than ever before!"
First, though, he sought to please his two new bosses,
Clipped, weeded, mowed, scrubbed mosses from the crosses
Stationed upon the convent's Calvary.
At length the ageing steward left him free
To organize his work at his own pace.
One day, in a secluded shady place,
Masetto saw two very young nuns peeping
Around a bush, assuming he was sleeping.
The day before they'd laughed till they were puce
Using the sort of words nice nuns don't use—
Which he, of course, pretended not to hear.
The bolder one said, "I've had an idea
I'd tell you if I thought you'd keep it quiet—
To add some spice to our dull daily diet
Of fasting, Latin prayers and meditation.
The hottest spice, they say, is copulation.
This big strong lad's deaf, mute and also dim:
So why not try how hot it is with him?"
The other gasped: "But what about our vows?
And what if we got pregnant?"—"Use your nous,"
The younger scoffed: "As long as no one knows,
What difference does it make?" After three goes
With M. behind the tool-shed, she confirmed
The truth of all she'd heard. The coy one squirmed

And dithered, but then—not to be outdone—
Next afternoon she also had her fun;
And from then on they missed no chance to enjoy
The age-old pleasures of their big new toy.
Until one day an older sister, viewing
The Tuscan landscape, spotted all three screwing
Like mad down at the bottom of the garden:
Amazed by dumb Masetto's hefty hard-on,
Her eyes alone asked two more sisters—brought
To witness this *ménage à trois*—what ought
They now to do: inform the abbess—or . . . ?
"Perhaps he'd welcome one or two nuns more,"
The shyest simpered, as they watched. And that
Knocked all their scruples into a cocked hat.
They waited till the three had finished dogging—
Giggling like blushing virgins, even snogging
A bit—and then went down to claim their share
In dim dumb strong Masetto: fair was fair.
The convent housed eight nuns in all, and so
Soon the remaining three were in the know.
They all took turns at riding hell-for-leather,
While staunch Masetto braced himself to weather
This storm of nuns, unholy and unholier.
Asleep one morning by the great magnolia,
Whose lemon-scented blossom filled the shade
With sweet, narcotic perfume—newly laid,
Masetto was observed by the abbess
In an embarrassing state of some undress,
And, though she was a serious-minded nun,
When he began to stiffen in the sun,
Dreaming no doubt of what he'd just been having,
Her gawp became a gaze, till the same craving
To which her younger charges had succumbed
Grabbed her as well. Her Bible was well-thumbed—
But no help now. Plucking him like a flower,

She woke and led him to her cell, or bower,
In whose snug privacy she dared to savour
The vice she'd always viewed with most disfavour,
For several days. The nuns soon comprehended
Why work on their own gardens was suspended
And, bitterly complaining to their Mother
Superior, failed to comfort one another.
But she and he ploughed on. And even if
Masetto's tool was less than keen or stiff,
She still knew how to get the greens she wanted.
Her gardener dug, drilled, seeded, puffed and panted,
Though in the flabby end, afraid lest he
Should do himself some serious injury,
He blurted out, "Please stop now, ma'am. I've heard
One cock will do for ten hens. But, no bird,
You need at least ten men! And here am I
Also required to serve and satisfy
Another eight. It's heaven on earth. But, please,
To carry on, I need to stand at ease
A little."—"Ha!" she gasped. "Why aren't you dumb?"
"I was, ma'am. But, you see, the more I've come
With you and all the other nuns, the less
I've felt stone-deaf and tongue-tied." The abbess,
Recalling how the sisters had been miffed
To lose their gardener, feeling somewhat biffed
By all these revelations, sat down quickly
But, in a moment, started smiling slickly—
Painfully aware that what was happening here
Could terminate her promising career.
Masetto smiled as well: the steward had died
Not long before—perhaps they could decide
On some arrangement which would suit them all?
If no one knew beyond the garden wall,
What difference would it make? And so their neighbours
Were told Masetto's prayers and saintly labours

Of horticultural love, plus the nuns' fasting
And holy tears, had moved the Everlasting
To unlock his tongue and open his blocked ears.
Masetto worked as steward for many years,
Helped by the nuns, and helped them in return
To lead a pleasant life and not to burn.
He also sometimes visited his wife,
Who was not unimpressed by his new life
Of prosperous piety. The girls and boys
He fathered were the secret pride and joy
Of all the convent, cared for by the nuns'
Families. Masetto raced his riotous sons
Around the garden, gave his daughters cherries—
Showed them where they could gather nuts, plums, berries,
And played at hide-and-seek . . . Till, finally,
The good abbess retired, and so did he,
Discreetly bribed with a fat monthly pension.
His wife now welcomed his well-off attention—
A sweet reversal of their former roles
(Though still involving neither of their souls)—
For she was hot, who used to be so cold,
"Though what," he wondered, "when she gets too old?"

iii

Nastagio degli Onesti and the Necromancer

In Trento, whose austere and gloomy church
Has weathered many centuries of strife,
Dispensing truth to souls afraid to search
For their own pathway through the woods of life,
There lived a youth who longed to have as his wife
A certain pious girl of noble stock;
But the more he told her so, the more she'd mock.

Rich as he was, this girl—a Traversari—
Treated him like a dog. His friends, appalled
At his declining health, declared it scary
To watch her tease him, till he cried or crawled . . .
Nastagio degli Onesti he was called.
He'd fallen in love, he said; and though it hurt,
You couldn't change your heart like you change your shirt.

As time went on, though, he became more bitter.
She grew as proper as a budding nun.
Not wishing to appear a fool or quitter,
He let offended pride sour all his fun.
His stubborn silence seemed to weigh a ton:
In fact, he looked hell-bent on self-destruction,
Dragged down by his love / hatred's swamp-like suction.

Secretly flattered but afraid and frigid,
She knelt in the family chapel, getting segs
On both cold knees. To her the rules seemed rigid:
Good works do not involve a youth who begs
To kiss you. *Re* the heat between her legs,
In which she was convinced her soul might burn, "O
Save me, dear Lord," she prayed, "from my own *Inferno!*"

Her girlfriends, getting married, asked her why
She treated him so harshly. With a cruel
Grin or grimace, she'd claim she'd rather die
Than marry a tin-pot commoner, the fool!
She often used a clyster when at stool;
Indulged in other nasty little habits;
And kept a stoat for hunting snakes and rabbits.

Sometimes she dreamt that she herself was hunted
By her father's howling pack of dogged dickers,
But always woke in time. Nastagio wanted
Above all things, she knew, to get his pickers
And feelers into what were not her knickers
Exactly but a sort of locking belt—
Where she herself quite often picked and felt.

After a year of so of this impasse
Nastagio, who had once been blithe and plump,
Felt like his nerves were stretched as thin as glass.
At last he puked his gripes in one big lump:
Unless she married him, he swore he'd jump
Into a romantic chasm in the Alps!
The hair stood up on both their prickly scalps.

"Then kill yourself," she shrilled: "See if I care!"
"My love," he bellowed, "if not consummated,
Will kill me anyway!" She swore: "I swear
Your love is nothing but brute lust, frustrated
By Jesus Christ, to whom I've consecrated
My life. I mean, my body and my soul
Are Jesus's, not yours. So shut your hole!

"You'll never have my body—not unless
You hunt me down with dogs and try to rape me.

My heart—unless you tear it from my breast—
Is His, not yours. I swear you'll never grope me.
Don't think your filthy fantasies escape me:
I know what men do. First of all you hump us—
And when you've had enough, you hate and dump us."

Speechless with shock, Nastagio left the town.
The Dolomites lay north and east of Trent.
His horse stopped in a wood where, dressed in brown
And vivid green, a young man stood. They went
Some way on foot: "My task is to prevent
You taking your own life," the stranger said.
"Life's short enough. We're all a long time dead."

It seemed that he could read Nastagio's mind.
He asked about old friends, but they were all
Long dead. They wept together. "Never mind
About the past, though. We survive or fall
Only here now. To belly-ache or bawl
Too much drowns heart and soul. Though fate proposes,
Each human being disposes . . .

But first some food and rest . . ." At once the trees
Became the doors and bookshelves of a room
Which opened into further libraries:
"My house is built of books—for some the tomb
Of history, but for me its brightest bloom.
The past is dead but should be with us, too:
I'll just call up a few dead souls for you."

—*Lucrece* came first, between her breasts the knife
Which might have done for *Tarquin*. With deep groans
She called on Jove to plague the rapist's life,
To make him moan: "Let no one hear his moans,
But stone him with hard hearts, harder than stones,

And let mild women lose their female mildness—
Wilder to him than tigers in their wildness.

"O give him time to think, and tear his hair!
O give him time to hate himself and rave!
Let him have time to wallow in despair.
Let him have time to groan as passion's slave.
Let him have time to beg, and cringe and crave,
And let the memory of his filthy crime
Have time to make his life a waste of time!"

—The next was *Troilus,* wishing he could die,
Looking so lean and feeble, pale and sick,
That no one knew him when he passed them by.
He felt so weak he used a walking stick.
Eating his heart out, drained and choleric,
If any old friend asked him where it hurt,
He answered it was in around his heart.

Nastagio heard him thinking. When he slept,
He saw his dreams: one afternoon he thought
That he was in a forest, where he wept
For her in whose hot snare his heart was caught.
And up and down he stalked and madly sought
Her in the sullen heat. But then he saw,
Asleep in the bright sun, a golden boar.

And in this big brute's arms, kissing his mouth
And silver tusks, lay lovely *Lady C.,*
As if the uncanny beast were her uncouth
Lord and master. When Troilus dreamt this, he
And poor Nastagio woke up suddenly:
"I'm dead already," each began to cry,
"Or, if not, why not?—Why can't I just die? . . ."

But next came that sweet peasant-girl, *Griselda,*
Waiting on her strange husband, *Marquis Walter,*
Who, testing her stoic fealty, cruelly held her
As helpless as a lamb on wedlock's altar.
But after all her trials he couldn't fault her.
Helpless, she helped herself. Powerless, her power
Was inwardly to bless and to endure.

Nastagio saw how, even as a marchioness,
Her soul was full of plain humility;
No expensive tastes, or over-touchiness,
No pomp, or imitation royalty:
Always benevolent and patient, she
Remained discreetly modest, full of kindness
Towards her powerful husband's wilful blindness . . .

—At last the necromancer clapped his hands,
Announcing that their revels now were ended,
Although he also issued soft commands
Resulting in a banquet, strangely attended
By magic shapes; the whole thing seemed suspended
By music in mid-air. He smiled at his guest:
"Lovers should try to eat, and also rest . . ."

After their meal Nastagio fell asleep,
And slept and dreamt of nothing all that night
And all the following day. As for the leap
He'd planned to take, to put himself in the right,
Into some dark abyss, when it grew light
On the third day, he woke and—lighter, too—
Asked his new *alter ego* what to do.

The necromancer told him he should bring
The girl to where his house and library stood,
Where she'd receive a valuable thing

Which he'd invoke in that enchanted wood:
A thing of more than usual flesh and blood,
And worth as much as they themselves were worth,
But buried, like their futures, in the earth . . .

At first, of course, she didn't want to come
But, in the end, sheer curiosity
Tempted her from her safe, ancestral home
Into the dirty wood. What might it be,
This precious thing she was to get or see?
Nastagio said he didn't have a clue:
Their host, no doubt, would tell them what to do.

When they arrived, both house and host were gone.
The girl accused him of a filthy trick
To get her in the wild woods on her own,
Confirming her belief that he was sick:
Just let him try, though—she could scratch and kick!
Needled, Nastagio finally lost his temper
And yelled at her to shut up or he'd thump her.

Instead of which she took a great deep breath
And started screaming madly. But then stopped.
The woods had turned as cold and dark as death.
Another woman screamed. Their hot hearts quopped
As, in the nude, the screamer flipped and flopped
Towards them through the undergrowth. A veil
Concealed her face. Her skin was torn and pale.

She seemed to be pursued by (invisible) hounds,
Whose teeth and claws she strove to push away
But which inflicted further gaping wounds
On back and legs while, shocked and helpless, they
Were forced to watch. She knelt and tried to pray

Just as a knight came crashing through the trees
On his black horse, and knocked her off her knees.

Swinging his axe, he seemed about to chop
The girl in pieces, when a virile shout
Clanged through the turgid air and made him stop.
Nastagio bravely clamoured: You great lout!
Try picking an opponent who can clout
You back! But he replied: Nastagio, look
In the black mirror of your life's closed book.

Nastagio looked, but couldn't see his face:
He wore an executioner's black hood.
He named the future time and nearby place
Where he'd chopped off his hand and let his blood
Soak back to earth. The girl had understood
With glee how much he loved her. Gratified,
Her ecstatic soul ate nothing till she died.

She'd hoped to go to heaven, whereas their hell
Was as Nastagio and his girl could see . . .
With that he raised his axe again. It fell
As if he were the girl's arch-enemy,
Splitting her bare back open. Groaning, he
Thrust his mailed fist into the darkest part
Of the huge wound, and grasped her pumping heart.

She died in terror, watching him pluck out
Heart, lungs and acrid entrails. He then threw
His dogs the whole hot heap. And she lay quiet
While he, in tears at what they had to do,
Waited and watched. The other pair wept too,
Until the dead girl sprang to her dead feet,
And the ritual time-loop started to repeat . . .

She raced off through the woods, pursued by the hounds,
The knight remounted and gave furious chase . . .
At last their host appeared, between two mounds
Which were their future graves. With gentle grace
He wiped the tears from her face and his face:
"Unless you want to die as hunter and quarry,"
He smiled, "agree to part in peace—or marry."

The Clouds dispell'd, the Sky resum'd its Light,
And Nature stood recover'd of her Fright.
But Fear, the last of Ills, remain'd behind,
And Horror sat on his Mind and her Mind.
She thought herself the trembling Dame who fled,
He thought himself the Ghost that spurr'd the Steed:
The downfal of her Empire she divin'd;
And his proud Heart with secret Sorrow pin'd.
Home as they went, the sad Discourse renew'd
Of the relentless Dame to Death pursu'd.
At ev'ry little Noise they look'd behind,
For still the Scene was present to their Mind . . .
Return'd, he took his Bed, with little Rest,
But in uneasy Slumbers dreamt the Worst:
She, forc'd to wake because afraid to sleep,
Her Blood all Fever'd, with a furious Leap
Sprung from the Bed, distracted in her Mind,
Till, desp'rate any Succour else to find,
She ceas'd all farther hope; and now began
To make reflection on th' unhappy Man.
Rich, Brave, and Young, who past expression lov'd,
Proof to Disdain; and not to be remov'd:
Of all the Men respected, and admir'd,
Of all the Dames, except her self, desir'd.
This quell'd her Pride, yet other Doubts remain'd,
That once disdaining she might be disdain'd:
The Fear was just, but greater Fear prevail'd,

Fear of her Life by hellish Hounds assail'd . . .
The welcom Message sent, was soon receiv'd;
'Twas what he wish'd, and hop'd, though scarce believ'd;
But she with such a Zeal the Cause embrac'd,
(As Women where they will, are all in hast)
That Father, Mother, and her Kin beside,
Were overborn by fury of the Tide:
With full consent of all, she chang'd her State,
Resistless in her Love, as in her Hate.

The Chest

"Apri questa cassa"—**Decameron VIII, viii**

Shortly before Boccaccio wrote, outside
The city-gates of Florence, on the road
To Fiesole, two well-known painters, who
'd been friends since early childhood, lived in two
Cottages where they shared a workshop and
Some goats—pigs—poultry on a patch of land,
Which they'd imagined would be all they needed
To work and play. Moreover, they'd succeeded,
By painting in the same style as each other,
In getting much of their main work together,
Frescoing villas—had, in fact, been doing
At Camerata one well worth the viewing
(As humorously recorded in a fine
If heartless story—No.5, Day 9),
Surrounded by tall Tuscan cypresses,
Vineyards and olive-groves—as it still is . . .
Bruno and Buffalmacco were their names,
Famous as well for zany fun and games,
Hoaxes and jokes, though only played on others:
As youths, they'd sworn to live and die as brothers.
They went to church to paint and not to pray,
But married in one on the same feast-day
Two girl-friends whom they'd known since they were little,
Playing at 'doctors' in their own 'hospital',
And so they'd lived as neighbours for some time.
That Easter Bruno went to paint in Rome,
Fulfilling every up-and-comer's dream
Of plying his brush in Giotto's top-notch team,
Although why one was chosen, not the other,
Was a hard question for his envious brother
Who, sourly, stayed to finish Camerata—

Returning, though, to his *Innamorata*
Each April evening. Bruno's wife would eat
Her supper with them, after the Spring heat
Had cooled, beneath the great magnolia tree
Which scented their whole courtyard. Until she,
After a lonely fortnight, feeling itchy,
Informed her friend she needn't be so bitchy
Just because she forgot to milk the goats!
Next day they jumped down one another's throats
About who should have fed the geese and ducks . . .
—*She's also far too noisy when she fucks*,
She thought, alone in bed: *Why don't they keep
Their window closed? Some people need their sleep!*—
But when she said so, felt herself go red,
Till Buffalmacco laughed: "It's hot in bed!"
A few days later, helping her to mend
A broken shutter, he watched her slowly bend
So far towards him that a breast flopped out
Of her loose bodice. With a pretty pout,
She pushed it back. He grinned: "I haven't seen
The other one for years! Perhaps fifteen?"
Vexed and confused at first—then thinking *Men!*—
She blushed, and smiled: "It's grown a bit since then . . ."
And, blushing deeper, lowered her bright eyes . . .
What happened next will come as no surprise
To readers of Boccaccio (whose narration
Seldom permits a pudibund translation,
While even an adaptation such as this is
Can hardly stop at unrequited kisses . . .),
Till Buffalmacco, being a young, well-fed,
Successful artist, loped from bed to bed,
Less discontented now to be at home
Instead of working wifelessly in Rome—
Contriving, too, that his own trusting wife
Saw nothing much. He led this lone wolf's life,

Keeping both women happy with no bother,
Till Giotto's pack, including his blood-brother,
Returned. *This can't go on,* both lovers thought.
The last time that they risked it they were caught,
If not exactly in the act, in doing
The sort of thing which quickly leads to screwing,
By Bruno's yellow eye, from where he sat
Drawing a sheep a field away: *Ha! What
In hell's name—?* Open-mouthed, he saw them move
Towards the bedroom: *Hey, they're making—!*
Deprived of words and movement, he sat on,
Plotting revenge, until the summer sun
Distracted him by setting with such beauty
That he forgot for several minutes his duty
As an offended male. When he came to,
The evening star was shining in dark blue.
And so he sloped off home, and shocked his wife
By brandishing a pointed boning knife,
Commanding her, on peril of her life,
To tell his faithless, good-for-nothing 'friend'
That he'd been called to Florence to attend
A funeral—would return the following day—
Which meant another chance for them, hurray.
"But once you've got him into bed, undressed,
You'll hear me hurrying back. The bedroom chest
Is big enough to hide him. Open that,
And lock him in it. Then we'll see what's what!"
And slammed the knife into the chest he meant,
Where it stood quivering. This great ornament
Had once belonged to Bruno's father, who
Had bought it cheap from someone that he knew
In Leghorn, where an English pirate had
Sold it, who'd got it from his English dad—
The English then being not as they are now,
Less decent and plain-dealing, anyhow . . .

But where the chest had come from no one knew.
The side that Bruno liked was mostly blue—
The sea, the sky, and Venus on a shell,
Her curves emerging from the waves' soft swell,
Crowned by red roses, looking sweetly scented,
While all around white flickering doves ascended.
Next to her you could see her blind son, Cupid,
Shooting the arrows which make people stupid,
And round the margins love-lorn knights—kings—queens,
And allegorical figures set in scenes
Of pleasure, hope, lust, falsehood, flattery,
Wasteful intrigue, with jaundiced Jealousy
Wearing a twisted wreath of marigolds and
Carrying a cuckoo, chained to her left hand . . .
The chest's original owner had preferred
Not to show Venus nude, or this mad bird,
But turned them to the wall—as Bruno turned
The other side, where Troy, for instance, burned
Under the auspices of blood-red Mars.
William of Raby, knighted in the wars
Against the French, had brought the chest from Paris
Together with a matching bed and arras,
Admiring their stern heroism, or
Stoic depiction of the world at war,
As he had known it—the fury and the clamour
Created by King Edward, as the hammer
Of Scotland, Wales and France . . . Thus Mars's temple
Of burnished steel and iron, for example,
Seemed built to last forever, while the god—
Armipotent, colossal—grimly stood
With a great red-eyed wolf at his bronze feet,
Which had been given a dying man to eat,
No doubt a Trojan soldier. William found
Homer's description of Troy's fate profound,
And all of Homer, come to that, sublime,

As true for William's as for any time
Before or after Ilium's loss of hope—
Including that of Alexander Pope,
Or even Dryden/Virgil's flattering slant
On empire-building heroes. Decadent,
Rapacious, proud, good enemy / bad friend,
Old Troy got its come-uppance in the end:
The fatal day, the appointed hour was come
When wrathful Jove's irrevocable doom
Transfers the Trojan state to Grecian hands.
The fire consumes the town, the foe commands;
And armed hosts, an unexpected force,
Break from the bowels of the fatal horse . . .
What tongue can tell the slaughter of that night?
What eyes can weep the sorrows and affright?
An ancient and imperial city falls;
The streets are filled with frequent funerals,
Houses and holy temples float in blood,
And hostile nations make a common flood.
All parts resound with tumults, plaints, and fears,
And grisly death in sundry shapes appears . . .
Thus William, with war-warped imagination,
Saw painted on the chest fair retribution
For what lewd Paris and his mates had done—
Helen avenged, Troy gutted in the sun—
But failed to notice, not being very observant,
The master murdered by his treacherous servant,
The stables burning with thick banks of smoke,
The smiler with the knife beneath his cloak,
The sow which ate a baby in its cradle,
The cook's hand scalded, *malgré* his long ladle,
A man who'd killed himself in utter despair—
His life-blood clotted in his yellow hair—
Or how a conquering hero on a throne
Sat in a tall dark tower all alone,

With a sword hanging right above his head,
Suspended by a thin and subtle thread . . .
All this was in the margins round the glory
Of Mars's temple and half-eaten, gory
Trojan. Which deeply suited William's mood
As he rode home. Though something of a prude,
He'd married, eighteen months or so before
He'd gone to screw the French in Edward's war,
The youngest daughter, *née* Elizabeth
Poole, of a local priest, whose sudden death
Had left her on her own. No one quite knew
What wealthy William thought he was up to
In taking this wild-eyed, red-lipped, black-haired
Wench as his wife—who'd never greatly cared
For girls before, whose tall and strait-laced mother
Thought boys should play with boys, not with the other
More frivolous sex . . . And yet Liz soon adjusted
To being a lady. Olive-skinned, big-busted
Yet slender, she had once been famous among
The village-children for her cat-like tongue,
Which easily touched the tip of her sweet nose,
For picking nuts up with her long brown toes,
And for her pointed teeth. As a young mis.,
She'd shown her girl-friends how the Frenchies kiss,
And licked them where it tickled. By the time
Her husband went to war, she'd had the time
To learn her Ps and Qs—and start to feel
Bored and frustrated, though each ample meal
She ate recalled how often she'd gone hungry.
William had dimly sensed that she was angry,
But rode to archery contests—jousted—hunted—
And shrugged it off as not knowing what she wanted,
Or eating too much meat. But, though a tall,
Good-looking husband, he was rather small
For her capacious, all too frequent wishes.

Once as a youth, when shooting bolts at fishes
Together with his friend, William de Ley,
At Raby Mere on a hot, sultry day,
They'd slid in from the boat and tried to swim.
He'd seen there was a difference between him
And his much slighter but well-hung companion,
But fended off the pang. In his opinion,
That sort of thing was not important. Willy,
As he was called—or, since some found this silly,
Will—was a youngest son, who hadn't married,
Nor would, he said, before his brothers buried
Themselves and he could more than swing a cat
(Liz stretched and smiled whenever she heard that)
Around the farm where he and they'd been born.
The friends were cousins and blood-brothers, sworn
To help each other—though all's fair in love
And war—especially in times of war and love,
For better or worse, in sickness and in health,
Regardless of their poverty or wealth . . .
Or so they'd vowed in the innocence of youth.
Also, of course, to tell each other the truth.
And apart from various milkmaids, shepherdesses,
And village virgins (one with coal-black tresses
And cat-like teeth), whom Willy didn't bother
To mention, they'd kept faith with one another—
Until their first real conflict *re* the war.
Willy's three brothers went. As No.4,
His business was to tend the family farm,
The three decided. Willy's weedy arm
Was not a warrior's (though at archery
No one could match the sharpness of his eye
Except, occasionally, William): i.e. they
Could better help the Hammer win the day.
Rich William had a steward (whose real name
Was not Malvoglio but, since cast in the same

Sour and efficient role, let's call him that),
Who'd run the estate and see to Liz the cat
While William rode in search of martial glory.
Fearing a nasty twist to their straight story,
Willy demanded William stay as well.
But William laughed out loud. *Then go to hell,
My friend,* thought Willy, also miffed to know
He'd lost the chance of shining with his bow,
As William would, he knew, and might get knighted,
While he, at home, remained ignored and slighted—
It wasn't fair. Liz listened to his case
With half-closed eyes. She found it a disgrace . . .
And yet was grateful for Will's company—
Too much alone since William was away . . .
What happened next soon made the sting of staying
Feel easier—and reminded him of laying
Her deep in Storeton Woods with nothing on
For half the day until the summer sun
Went down that whole hot June before she married . . .
Not that they saw their oaths as dead and buried,
But in abeyance for as long as (they
Agreed) his friend / her husband stayed away.
Later all oaths were to be reinstated.
Or so they reasoned. But, so long frustrated,
Lizzy, *née* Poole, began to fall in love—
At least, could hardly ever have enough
Of Will before she wanted him again.
And he performed like half-a-dozen men.
Her eighteen months of boredom, put to flight,
Had left her with a ravening appetite,
Also for meat and drink. And many a feast
Of roasted loin or heart of hunted beast
And strong red wine concluded their long sessions,
Or opened them again. To hide their passions
Was not that easy. William had a page,

Whose job it was to tend his equipage
At jousts and archery contests. Cherubino—
Let's call him that—became their go-between. O
Heartless disloyalty of adolescence,
Obsessed with hair-do's, pimples and tumescence!
The more Liz teased this boy's sweet dick the faster
He zipped between them and forgot his master—
Too young for France but not to hide and peep,
Which Liz allowed for helping them to keep
Their trysts a secret from Malvoglio, who
Was not a fool, though, and already knew
What was afoot, but chose to bide his time
Rather than face two lovers in their prime . . .
After twelve months (and how were they to end
Such loving then?) her husband / his best friend
Returned from France, where he had had to quell an
Unpleasant feeling she might be a Helen,
Not a Penelope, though in his dreams
The niggle burrowed on, like hidden streams
He did his best to ignore. Thus this straight man,
Who always finished what he had begun,
And had entirely trusted his straight mother,
Tried hard—one woman being much like another—
To trust his wife. And brought the bed, plus chest
And arras home. But, then, his steward confessed
He'd smelt a rat—though, fearing for his life,
He'd not yet dared confront Sir William's wife
With *who* exactly slithered to and fro
When they presumed he wasn't there. And so
The matter hung. After so much spilt blood,
Sir William was in grim, Homeric mood.
Though his heart sank, he quietly swore he'd kill
Anyone who betrayed him, even Will.
Not that his friend would ever let him down,
But from the lowest beggar to the crown,

Fear of retaliation was what kept
The world in order. Even while you slept,
The greater fear of what might happen when
The deed was done deterred nine out of ten
Murderers, adulterers, thieves, and other rabble,
And helped to keep most people out of trouble.
Without such fear most soldiers would desert.
Punishments must be seen, and seen to hurt.
"Yes, yes," Malvoglio slobbered. "And the best
Place to find out who's who is madam's chest.
But should not you, sir, be the first to know
Whoever is your good wife's gigolo?
When Cherubino slinks across the fields . . ."
Another blow. But which good steward shields
His master from the truth? Malvoglio blurted
It all out now—how often C.'d deserted
His post to pimp for Liz, how often she'd
Been busy, morning, noon and night, when he'd
Had business to discuss—"And, by the way,
That little dog has more than had his day
At playing Peeping Tom! . . ." A few days later
William was back in France, the perpetrator
Of three bad ends. Crammed in the chest, he'd knelt
Or lain, and heard and seen, until he felt
Like a Greek waiting in the Trojan horse,
Or spare prick at a wedding. Or, of course,
A foetus huddling in its mother's womb,
And, lastly, like a corpse shut in a tomb,
Or dead heart in his own unfeeling chest.
Speechless and stunned, he felt as though the best
Of life was over. But what should he do?
Hours passed. Then he recalled they'd planned to go
To Chester on the following day to shoot
In an archery contest. In the woods *en route*—
Down in dark Dibbensdale, where William knew

No one would see what he now planned to do—
The traitor Cherubino suffered the fate
Of false Melanthius, barred inside the gates
Of Ithaca, who'd turned his coat to please
The suitors, and abandoned Ulysses
To his ill luck: *His zealous men fulfil*
At every point their master's rigid will:
First bind his hands and feet behind his back
And hoist him by the rope, till his joints crack,
Into a tree, where his own writhing weight
Causes the splintering bones to dislocate.
The howling felon swung from side to side—
Until they gagged him. Then they left him tied
And tortured in mid-air, awaiting Will,
Who soon came cantering down the wooded hill.
He stopped in horror when he saw the page,
Two hooded men, and William white with rage.
But, frowning grimly, with a dreadful look
That withered Willy's heart, his best friend spoke:
"Dog, you have had your day! To England's shore
You hoped her husband would return no more."
William had fetched his father's great long-bow,
Which only he could draw. He drew it now—
Almost as if, before his friend lay dead,
The immortal lines went shooting through his head:
And now the famous bow Ulysses bore,
Turned on all sides, inspecting it before
He strung it lest time's worms had done it wrong,
Its owner absent, and unused so long . . .
Then, as a minstrel strings anew his lyre
Or fits the dumb lute with a singing wire,
Relaxing, straining, drawing to and fro,
So the great master drew the mighty bow,
And drew with ease—until the string, let fly,
Twanged short and sharp, like the shrill swallow's cry.

Swift as a word, the parting arrow sings,
Bearing the sting of death on its black wings:
Full through the throat Ulysses' weapon passed—
And pierced Will's neck. He fell and breathed his last,
With streams of dark blood gushing from his head
And severed veins. A puddle quickly spread
Around him on the ground. But, not content,
William attacked the corpse, as if he meant
To kill it twice—cut open Willy's chest—
Tore out his treacherous heart—and flung the rest
As carrion to the crows now circling round.
Next they dropped Cherubino to the ground,
Who'd seen all this, cut off his nose and ears
And voyeur's genitals with shepherd's shears
And fed them to the dogs, which wolfed them down
Before the boy had ceased to cry and groan:
His hands and feet last felt the cruel steel,
He roar'd, and torments gave his soul to hell . . .
Returning home at once, Sir William took
The heart, wrapped up in leaves, to his French cook,
As if it were the heart of a wild boar,
Requesting him to mince it and prepare
The finest and most succulent dish he knew.
The cook produced a bowl of rich *ragoût*.
That evening Liz and William dined alone.
William felt sick. Liz ate the stew on her own.
She'd always had an excellent appetite.
Her husband watched her, turning deathly white:
The heart, he hoped, had pleased her as much dead
As when it was alive. "What's that you said?"
She almost spat, afraid of his strange look.

*

What happened next depends which poem or book
You're reading. Or on how high/low you think

This Mars or Venus might ascend or sink:
Whether, like Tosca from Sant' Angelo,
Liz would defy her fate and nobly throw
Herself from the high window of the tower
They found her mangled body under—or,
Backing away from him in horror and fear,
She didn't think the window was so near,
And simply tripped—or whether he intended
Only to slap or beat her up but ended
By losing all control until he pushed
Her hissing and spitting out. The sheer drop crushed
Her head and limbs so badly no one could tell
What happened in the tower before she fell.
Except that, just before she toppled from it,
She left behind a cat-like pool of vomit . . .
Afraid of Will's two brothers (one was dead)
And Cherubino's family, William fled
By ship the following morning from Parkgate
To Plymouth and then France. Filled with self-hate
After a night of contemplating what
He'd done—but they deserved all that they got,
Surely?—he cursed his friend, but never told
Anyone how Liz fell. Malvoglio sold
The arras, chest, and desecrated bed . . .
—Before the year was out, William was dead.

*

The bed was separated from the chest—
And, later, itemized "my second-best"
By another well-known William in his will.
The arras hung around in Stratford, till
Its worn remains were carted to the Globe
Where it served to carpet throne-rooms, make a robe
Or a furred gown, and be the actual arras
Which helped another vengeful blade embarrass

His relatives (and lug his victim's guts
From then to now) with all the ifs and buts
Which he or Will could think of . . . But the chest,
More than two hundred years before, sailed west
With other warlike pirates down the Dee
And south to Leghorn in hot Tuscany,
Then on to Florence, where our tale began—
And where, meanwhile, another unhappy man
Was hiding in it. Buffalmacco knelt
Or lay stretched out, like William, till he felt
The chest begin to jerk, and even creak,
With the unaccustomed weight, for an antique,
Of Bruno's tit for tat on its flat top.
Poor Buffalmacco thought they'd never stop.
And when they stopped, they started off again—
Sighing and grunting as if in sweet pain—
Just minutes later. Bruno's unhappy wife,
Who'd co-produced this intermarital strife,
Was listening too, outside the bedroom door.
Bruno had sent her, as a punishment for
Deceiving him, to undeceive her friend,
Who, he suggested, might keep up her end
By doing as she'd been done by. To save face,
He hoped to implicate her, and disgrace
The three of them in private . . . *What a cow!*
Thought Buffalmacco's wife. Then showed them how
To keep your end up for an hour or more.
Bruno lost count of *her* orgasms, but four—
Or was it five?—was his own personal best
At breakfast-time. They did it on the chest
(She thought) because her neighbours' marriage-bed—
The idea of which kept running through her head—
By then had been sufficiently defiled,
Which made her blood run hot and very wild.
She ended up, as Bruno flagged, on top—

But when he limply signalled her to stop,
She twisted round to *soixante-neuf* instead
And came again while sitting on his head.
Her very last was a DIY job,
Concluding with deep groans and then a sob,
Which Bruno found unnerving. Such excessive
Female excitement made him feel quite passive—
But, leaping from the chest, he lugged his wife
Into the room and, grasping the long knife
With which he'd frightened her, and which had lain
Unseen beside them, frightened her again
By pointing at the chest without a word.
As if (while her friend sobbed) she hadn't heard
The whole performance, sighs and sobs and all,
And ground her teeth and cursed them through the wall,
She laughed and passed it off with "Well, my dears,
You've paid me back in kind all right. And here's"—
Unlocking and then lifting up the lid—
"Another who's been done by as he did."
If Buffalmacco had not felt so harassed,
He might have laughed to see his wife embarrassed
So cleverly by Bruno's practical joke,
Who'd laid her as if lying on her bloke.
But that was *him!* And, more undressed than dressed,
He virtually vaulted out of William's chest.
All four then stood there wondering what to do,
Bruno in dubious triumph, and the two
Women not knowing what to hope or fear,
Till Buffalmacco had a bright idea:
"My friends, we've known each other for so long,
And shared so much, I think it would be wrong
To be tight-fisted when it comes to love.
So why not share our spouses? Why not have
Two each, in other words? Each man two wives,
Each woman two men, living out our lives

In harmony and friendship till the end?" . . .
And so wife shared with wife and friend with friend,
Nor did this new arrangement ever lead
To arguments or jealousy. Indeed,
Since jealous thoughts can turn a heaven to hell,
They all felt happier. Which is just as well,
And of imaginable endings seems the best,
Thus wrapping up these stories of the chest.
Two somewhat plainer versions may be found
Adorning *The Decameron's* fertile ground—
Though who can tell now if Boccaccio knew
Or cared if either one of them were true?

The Gift

*"My name might be Cromwell,
Not just Bill Jackson!
She boycotts me, protesting
Protestant, Anglo-Saxon."*

*

Oliver Cromwell lay buried and dead,
Until the new king's men
Declared he should pay for the old king's blood,
And dug him up again.

They dragged him publicly through the streets
From Westminster Abbey, and hung
His carcass up like a common thief;
The common people flung

Brickbats and mud at his winding sheet.
As though he were still not dead,
The hangman cut him down again
And chopped off his stubborn head.

The Tyburn hangman hacked off his head
With eight cloth-muffled blows.
And so the new king had his way
With the Old One's 'Lancaster rose'.

They chopped off his fingers, his nose and and ear
And threw his trunk in a pit.
But they kept his shaven head—to do penance
As the king and his men saw fit . . .

From a spike high up on Westminster Hall
Oliver's head looked down—
On the time-serving merchants and bankers
Of a richer and safer town,

Where prudence, self-interest, piety and thrift
Loved *More* and hated *Less*—
Whipped beggars, seeking Justification
In Industry and Success.

Reviewing thus his lifetime's work,
Oliver groaned and wept
In self-disgust and disenchantment;
And when at last he slept

He dreamt he was hunting two grey wolves
Across the Irish Sea;
His favourite daughter, returned from the dead,
Rode with him fierily.

They raced through the stormy air till they heard
The songs of a twangling isle,
Where they stopped. An old man welcomed them
Who had a young man's smile.

His songs turned slowly into a dirge,
And, slowly, he grew as young
As Oliver's daughter. His smile became
As old and strange as the spring.

The daughter thought, "If this young man
Will only sing for me,
I'll love him forever with all my heart."
But he sang on carelessly.

She sighed and thought, "If this young man
Will only lie with me,
I'll do whatever he likes best."
But he turned and walked away.

She thought at last, "If this young man
Will only marry me,
He shall be richer than the sun."
But his eyes flashed dangerously.

She said, "Your eyes are green as the grass
On my father's richest land—"
But her clothes turned into beggars' rags,
And he placed his green eyes in her hand.

The eyes turned into emeralds
As bright as a soldier's sword.
But she buried them next to the broken bones
Of their dead without a word.

From the eyes two trees sprang up through the bones,
Whose branches grew into each other.
Now Oliver saw the man as his son—
His daughter, as her brother.

Oliver gave him his daughter as wife.
She died giving birth. A girl's sight
Soon blest her father's homeward path
Into the vanishing light.

*

Oliver Cromwell lay buried and dead,
Heigho! buried and dead!
There grew a green apple-tree over his head,

Heigho! over his head!
The apples were ripe and all ready to drop!
Heigho! ready to drop!
There came an old woman to gather the crop,
Heigho! gather the crop!

Rainer Maria Rilke: A Post-Romantic Portrait (On Poetry and Death)

"O sage, Dichter, was du tust?"

i

Early Apollo

As sometimes, when the woods are dry and leafless,
A dawn looks through them that's already bright
With Spring: so there is nothing in this griefless
Face which could shade the almost fatal light

To which all Poetry might here expose us.
For there's no shadow yet in how he sees,
His head's too cool for bay-leaves, and the roses
Will only later grow as tall as trees

And form a garden out of his old brows
Whose single, fallen leaves, when song or hymn
Bursts from his lips, will move where his mouth blows,

Which is still silent—pristine and still gleaming—
And, smiling, drinks in something which comes streaming
As if all song were entering him.

ii

Song of the Women to the Poet

Look, how the whole world opens! So do we.
For we are nothing if not blessed. Our souls

Were bestial blood and darkness—until they
Took root in us as soul, which howls

And cries out still. And cries now soulfully
For you—who take, it seems, a gentle view
Of us as landscape. And your face is free
Of lust or greed. Which means it can't be you

For whom it howls. And yet aren't you the one
Where we might wholly lose ourselves?—Why fear it?
And how could we be *more* in anyone?

With us, it passes—this infinity.
But you, now, be—you Mouth—so that we hear it;
But you now, you Us-sayer: you now be.

iii

The Death of the Poet

He lay there, his uplifted countenance
Pale with denial in its pile of cushions,
Now that the world, torn from his sense impressions,
With all his knowledge of its forms and fashions,
Had lapsed into the year's indifference.

No one who saw him there could guess
How much he'd been at one with all existence;
For *this*—these depths, these meadows, this persistence
Of water—this in fact *was* his real face.

And, oh, his face was all that—far and wide—
Approaches now as if to court him here;
Whereas his mask, which passes on in fear,
Is soft and open as the inner side
Of fruit, which decomposes in the air.

iv

L'Ange du Méridien

(*Chartres*)

With all the force of nihilistic thought,
A tempest tests this huge cathedral's strength;
And so it's with a sense of something sought
That we're attracted by your smile at length,

O feeling angel, by your gentle smile
Whose mouth is sculpted from a hundred mouths . . .
But are you aware—or not—of how our hours
Slip from the fullness of your dial,

Whose figures show the whole day's total, which,
Equally real, are balanced there as fully
As if all hours were ripe and rich.—

What *do* you, stone one, know of our Being's plight,
Turning, perhaps, with deeply, even wholly
Ecstatic looks, your sun-dial towards the night?

v

Morgue

They lie here, as if waiting to be told,
Belatedly, some tale to reconcile them
To one another and to this deep cold,
Some plot or plan to enliven or inspire them;

For nothing here has ended, nothing has changed.
What sort of names—for which undying truths—
Are found in inside pockets? Someone has washed
The worn-out sadness round their mouths,

But failed to shift it; cleaned it, anyhow.
Their beards still sprout, the bristles somewhat harder
But tidied up—whose conscientious warder

Spares starers any sickness or surprise . . .
Behind their weary eyelids their cold eyes
Have turned, until they're looking inward now.

vi

The Panther

(*In the Jardin des Plantes, Paris*)

Bars pass and pass. His gaze no longer rages
But, utterly tired, can't hold things any more.
He sees a thousand bars. Beyond his cage's
Bar after bar, no other world is there.

His soft lithe slouch hunts down no weak tormentor
But, circling on and on with short sharp turns,
Is like a dance of power around a centre
In which his great dazed will no longer burns.

Sometimes, the curtains of his pupils sliding
Open, a silent image soothes his eyes—
Enters his tense, still bulk. Till, swiftly gliding
Into his heart, it dies.

vii

The Gazelle

(*Gazella Dorcas*)

Enchanted one, how can the sound of two
Selected words ever achieve the rhyme
Which comes and goes in you, like beating time?
Your lyre-like horns ascend as if leaves grew

On them—and all about you has so often
Figured in songs of love, which soothe and soften
Like roses' petals on the closed eye-lids
Of a reader who no longer reads

In order to see *you,* borne there as though
Each run were fully loaded with long leaps
Which wait to shoot away just so

Long as your neck's alert, like one who keeps
On breaking off her woodland swim to take
A look who else is swimming in her lake.

viii

The Unicorn

The saint looked up. And prayer slipped from his mind
As a helmet falls from the head—distracted
By the silent, unbelieved-in, never-expected
Animal drawing near like an abducted,
Helplessly pleading, all-white, wide-eyed hind.

The creature's long, stiff legs of ivory-white
Moved forward with an easy, balanced tread;
A blessed gleam went gliding through its coat,
And on its lucid, peaceful, beast's forehead
Its horn shone like a tower in bright moon-light,
And rose as each step forward raised its head.

The mouth, beflecked with rosy, greyish foam,
Was puckered, and the white teeth, shining through—
Whiter than all—gleamed in the glade's pale glow.
The slightly panting nostrils noticed who
Was there, whereas its gaze, which no
Object restricts, cast visions on the gloom,
Weaving a saga cycle in deep blue.

ix

Saint Sebastian

Standing up like someone lying down,
Force of will alone can have supported
This . . . As nursing mothers are transported—
Self-involved—he wreathes himself a crown.

Arrows come—here—now—as if
Springing from his loins. But, unastounded,
Darkly smiling still, he seems unwounded
As their quivering shafts grow stiff.

Only once his sorrows grow,
And his eyes expose his suffering, though
Soon reject again as merely petty—
And contemptuously let go—
Such destroyers of a thing of beauty.

x

Portrait of my Father as a Young Man

The dream-filled eyes. The brow's strong predilection
For far-off things. About the mouth enorm-
ous youth, and unused smiles of seduction,
And—posed before the braided, laced perfection
Of the tightly fitting, noble uniform—
The sabre's knuckle-guard and both hands, which
Are quiet and wait, not pushing and not pushed—
And, now, almost invisible. As if such
As touch the distance vanish. And
The whole is veiled within itself—and hushed—
And dimmed as if we couldn't understand;
And its deeply clouded depths hold out no hope.—

You quickly fading old daguerreotype
In my more slowly fading hand.

xi

Self-Portrait from the Year 1906

An ancient, aristocratic ancestry,
Whose eyebrows' arches brook no compromise.
The fears of childhood still in his blue eyes,
And here and there a deep humility.—
A servant's. Or a woman's. No stable-boy's.
The mouth formed as a mouth, large and precise—
Not to persuade but state what's just, what's free.
The forehead without guile, contentedly
Shadowed and bowed in spiritual exercise.

These scattered features time will make or mar,
Which have not yet been fully concentrated
By suffering or success, or penetrated
To lasting goals. Yet a real face seems fated
To come together here, as if from far.

xii

The Last Graf von Brederode Escapes from Turkish Imprisonment

They followed, shooting multicoloured death
From far behind him. Lost and terrified, he
Fled on, aware of nothing but the threat
He fled from, while his far-off ancestry

Appeared as nothing now: hunted by men,
Even a beast will flee. Until, at the side
Of a flashing, roaring river, the will to decide
Raised him above distress, turned him again—

As if among fine ladies, smiling sweetly—
Into a princely son of royal blood:
They smiled upon his radiant face, completely

Fulfilled—so young. Great-hearted, on he rode
Aglow with blood. And his horse bore him greatly—
As into his own castle—into the flood.

xiii

The Carousel

(Jardin du Luxembourg)

Rotating in the shade of its bright roof,
For a little while this gaily coloured stand
Of horses from the slowly vanishing land
Of childhood moves, though they don't move a hoof.
Though some are hitched to coaches, they don't pant;
But all of them have brave and eager faces.
A fierce red lion puts them through their paces,
And now and then a pure white elephant.

As if through trees, a stag swings into view,
Wearing a bridle, reins and saddle, where
A little girl is buckled, dressed in blue.

And, on the lion, a boy—not yet a youth—
Rides white and holding tight with one small hand.
The lion itself exhibits tongue and tooth.

And now and then a pure white elephant.

And, on their horses, riding through the air
They come; and fair-haired girls who—if the truth
Were told—are too mature for such uncouth
Horse-jumping, looking here, there, anywhere—

And now and then a pure white elephant.

And so it hurries past to its conclusion,
And whirls and circles on without an aim.
Reds, greens and greys in colourful profusion;
A profile, hardly worthy of the name;
Sometimes a smile, as if in sweet collusion,
Still dazzling—blessed—and wasted on the illusion
Of this blind, breathless game . . .

xiv

Spanish Dancer

As in the hand, before it really burns,
A match's sulphur head, from all sides, sends
Out white-hot, flickering tongues, so now she turns
In quick, bright, flickering circles, hotly warns
Her audience back to where the dance extends.—

And suddenly the whole full flame is there.

And, with a single look, she lights her hair;
Abruptly turns, and sets her dress alight
With daring art, and heated appetite;

And raises naked arms like rattling snakes,
Which her fire-dance alarms—and now awakes.

And then, as if the fire were burning low,
She gathers it all up—only to throw
It proudly down, and gestures proudly, glaring
At where it hits the ground, still madly flaring
And raging on, consuming time and space . . .
But now, assured of victory, with a sweet
Familiar smile, she raises her fine face,
And stamps it out with powerful little feet.

xv

Archaic Torso of Apollo

We never saw or heard the numinous head
Whose eyeballs blazed like apples ripely growing.
But still his torso's somewhat softer glowing,
As of a branching street-lamp, holds instead

The brilliance of his look. Or how could the prow
Of his breast blind you? Or the subtle turning
Of his loins light a smile and send it burning
Into the procreative centre? How

Could he not seem disfigured, not seem short
Beneath the shoulders' fallen nought?
Or shimmer like a predator's bright fur?

Or break forth, like a star which seems to strive
Beyond its bounds? For there's no place from where
He cannot see you. You must change your life.

xvi

Leda

The swan the great god entered in his need
Shocked him—or almost shocked him—by its beauty;
Confused, he disappeared in it completely,
But then, concealed, was driven to the deed

Before he'd even tried to probe or plot
Its unknown *Dasein*. And she—the opened one—
Realized at once who'd come disguised as a swan,
And knew at once: he wanted what—

Confused, unable to withstand
His will—she couldn't cover. Moving lower,
And necking past her weakening hand,

Into his love the god released soul's sap—
And, only then at one with its white power,
Became pure swan in her loved lap.

xvii

Corrida

(In memoriam Montez, 1830)

Since he lightly burst from the toril,
Almost small, with startled eyes and ears,
Taking on the stubborn picadors
And the banderillas—look, the bull

Like a storm-cloud has increased
To a massive, black, accumulated
Hatred, as of all he's hated—
Clenched his head into a fist,

Taking nothing now from any man
Lightly: now, with bloody banners showing
Over lowered horns, obscurely knowing—
Having *always* been against the one

Who, in his embroidered, pink silk-suit
Quickly turns and, like a black bee-swarm,
Lets the deeply consternated brute
Pass beneath his mauve and golden arm—

Raising easily misdirected, hot
Eyes again towards his still ungored
Rival who, performing on the spot
Chiaroscuro circles without thinking,
Till the bull stands blindly blinking,

Now prepares—serene, unhurried, calm,
Cool, and leaning forward on his arm
Over that on-coming, great
Wave with all its thrust of wasted hate—
Almost gently to insert his sword.

xviii

Saint George

On her frightened knees all night,
Weak and wakeful, "Look," the virgin

Called, "a watchful dragon,"—urging
Him to come and solve her plight:

"Why guard *me?*" On his pale horse,
In his glorious suit of armour,
Bursting forth, to cheer and charm her,
Like the dawn—a brilliant force,

Up to whom, still kneeling, she
Gazed: along the downs he thundered
Brightly, raising his two-handed
Weapon, much too dangerously,

And too dangerous, even though,
Praying harder, as a woman
On her helpless knees, she'd summoned
Him to save her—could not know

How her heart, so pure and willing,
Dragged him down from God's heaven-filling
Light. Her prayers, while he was killing,
Grew as tall as towers can grow.

xix

Turning Point

"The way from deep feeling to greatness is through sacrifice."—Kassner

Looking had long been his glory.
Stars would drop to their knees,
Wrestled there by his gazing.
Or, if he knelt to look,

Even the gods grew weary
Breathing his powerful incense;
Smiled at him in their sleep.

Towers he would look at until—
Frightened—they shook;
Building them up again, quickly, in one!
Yet how often the landscape,
Heavy laden with day,
Rested at last in his peaceful awareness, evenings.

Animals, trustful, moved
Into his open gaze,
Grazing. The captive lions
Stared, as at inconceivable freedom.
Birds went flying through him—
Straight through his soul; and flowers
Looked again in his eyes, as
Large as in children.

And rumours that someone was *looking*
Moved all the less, the
Questionably visible,
Moved the women.

How long looking?
How long inwardly lacking—
Pleading from deep in his eyes?

While he sat waiting, away from home; a hotel's
Distracted, averted bed-room
Sullen around him, and in the evaded mirror
Again the hotel-room
And, later, from the miserable bed

Again:
Consultations held in air,
Incomprehensible consultations—
Over his feeling heart,
Over his heart which in spite of his pain-racked
Body still made itself felt—
Were taking place and deciding:
That it had no love.

(And denied him greater glory.)

For there's a limit, you see, to looking.
And the well-looked-at world
Wishes to flourish in love.

Work of the face is done,
Now do heart-work
On the images captured within you; for you
Overpowered them: but now you don't know them.
Look, inner Man, at your young inner Woman,
At the one you have won from
A thousand natures, at
The creature you've still only won, the
Never yet loved one.

xx

Sonnet to Orpheus

A tree ascends! O unimpaired transcendence!
O Orpheus sings! O high tree in the ear!
And all grew silent. Yet in that deep silence
New bearings, and new clues, and change were there.

Creatures of stillness crowded from the clear,
Relaxing wood—from nest and hiding place;
Till soon it seemed their inner quiet, their grace
Of movement came from neither greed nor fear

But from their listening. There in that bright clearing,
The howls, shrieks, roaring in their hearts felt small.
And so, with scarcely shelter to receive it—

A burrow or den, as dark desires conceive it,
With quivering door-posts and an earthen wall—
Your song created temples in their hearing.

xxi

(Rilke's Epitaph)

Rose, oh pure contradiction, desire
To be no one's sleep under so many
Eyelids.

TRANSLATOR'S COMMENTARY *(2007)*

Of another poem from the time when most of the above were composed, Joseph Brodsky wrote in his essay, 'Ninety Years Later', "Written in 1904, 'Orpheus. Eurydice. Hermes' by Rainer Maria Rilke makes one wonder whether the greatest work of the century wasn't done ninety years ago". Beginning in the 1930s and '40s, Rilke's appeal (one might almost speak of popularity) in English-speaking countries has continued to increase as time goes on—such that, as Brodsky says, "translating Rilke has become practically a fad". Other readers (and translators) will have other explanations but I can think of three reasons for this—two good and one not so good—which the above translations incidentally illustrate while building up their admittedly selective (and perhaps still unfinished) picture of the poems' original author . . . Walter Benjamin once claimed that one of his ambitions was to produce a work made up entirely of quotations. One species of quotation can consist, fairly obviously, of various sorts of translation. In the case of Rilke, one can quote the form of the poetry as well as its sense, since German and English (unlike French or Italian, for example) are relatively 'stress-timed' or isochronous languages and the significance or 'feel' of Rilke's metres and stanzas is the same as or very similar to that of their English equivalents. Which is, moreover, another way of saying that if any of the translations are valid as poetry, the main reason, as Brodsky insisted, "is, in the first place, of course, Rilke himself" . . .

The first and most obvious reason, then, for Rilke's appeal is the strikingly high proportion—even for a poet of his acknowledged status—of what Eliot called "genuine poetry" in his work. In spite of the compression and difficulties of some of his syntax and much of his thought, Rilke validates over and over again Eliot's claim "that genuine poetry can communicate before it is understood". As in the case of Dante, whom Eliot was writing about, Rilke's poetry can do this in spite of a reader's poor grasp of the language of the original or poor translations. In *Neue Gedichte*, in particular, this "direct shock of poetic intensity", as Eliot describes it, has much to do with Rilke's virtuoso handling of metre and rhyme and also with the play of his syntax within and across his lines and stanzas, as I have tried to show in the translations. The striking physicality of the poems' images, their extraordinary condensation *("Dichten = condensare",* as Pound famously if inaccurately condensed it) and the mature Rilke's genius for selecting *le mot juste* are other elements involved. At any rate, the original poems are frequently "breathtaking" (Brodsky's epithet), and every *aficionado* of Rilke will remember which lines or which poem grabbed him first—and, once grabbed, as Eliot says, "nothing but laziness can deaden the desire for fuller knowledge".

The second reason I can think of for Rilke's appeal may be that, having gone on to consider what the poetry is both more specifically and more generally about, one finds, again, a strikingly high proportion of emotional and spiritual truth or wisdom. The spiritual sort, in particular, is so unusual in Anglophone poetry that once the reader has been "exposed" (see 'Early Apollo') to the light of poems like '*L'Ange du Méridien*', 'The Unicorn' or 'Archaic Torso of Apollo'—to mention three favourites of my own—Eliot's "desire for fuller knowledge" is frequently excited all the more. Like a lot of exciting or shocking or otherwise memorable experiences ("Poetry isn't, as people imagine, merely feelings," Rilke wrote in *Malte Laurids Brigge*, "it is experiences"), this sort of poem often feels new but also familiar. One reason for this may be that, although he can be looked on as the consummation, or ultimate apotheosis, of European Romanticism (after which it could only decline—and has, with one or two exceptions), Rilke also went *beyond* Romanticism in that he pursued the subjective into what are virtually objective regions of emotional and spiritual observation. Of course, there is no observation without an observer, but let's say he arrived at and operated on a level of consciousness whereby he was able to see and write of emotional and spiritual realities which we really do seem to have in common. Patrick Bridgwater in the introduction to his excellent translation of *Duino Elegies* (1999) quotes Rilke as having written in 1920, "Art can proceed only from a purely anonymous centre." In theory, Rilke is an élitist, of course, but in practice virtually anyone can recognize his meanings in themselves. This is, for me, the very heart of 'Post-Romanticism'—the realization or (as Rilke would have it) *experience* of the fact that the innermost self is not a personal identity but a nameless and even numinous impulse which we have in common. *"Namenlos bin ich dir entschlossen"*— "Namelessly I am committed to you"—he wrote in *Duino Elegies* IX, and the life-blood of this commitment, for Rilke but also for anyone, is the *Dasein* we may "seek to become"—the existential freedom (as it came to be known) not merely to react but to decide, not merely to be formed but to transform, not to evade but to subsume, not to blame but to praise.

The third and more dubious—if understandable—reason for Rilke's popularity is also related to his Romanticism. Rilke, like everyone else, was a man of his age, and it is perhaps not very surprising, given the general cast of his mind, that the characteristic withdrawals and self-assertions of the Romantic reaction to the 'Dual Revolution', as Eric Hobsbawm called it, of the late 18th and 19th centuries are also easy to find in or read into his writing, which can easily be taken, in other words, as bearing gifts to the escapist or even solipsist in all of us—as Auden presumably meant by describing him (ambivalently) in his *New Year's Letter* (1940) as "the Santa Claus of loneliness". Of course, Auden and Rilke (for all the former's admiration of the latter's artistry) were very different sorts of poet, and the question of writerly intent and readerly attribution is more than usually tricky with regard to Rilke. Even so, if it is true, as *Poetry Review* 95:3 recently put it, that "A New Age Rilke would not be Rilke at all, of course", his conspicuous lack of interest in, or withdrawal from, almost everyone's everyday life—the world of work, for obvious example, but also family life and other social and political realities—is perhaps his most serious limitation. At the same time, it is much less of a problem, one sometimes feels, in the world which his poetry creates, to view the artist and especially the poet as a kind of hero or inspired seer than it is in the world which most of us have to cope with day by day. Presumably because his mind was for the most part so intent on higher things, Rilke could also be surprisingly heartless . . . Of course, every reader will decide for him- or herself about the actual value of Rilke's values but, for all his emotional and spiritual acumen, he remained relatively indifferent to questions of ethics. And yet in the absence of a shared ethic, whose emotional or even spiritual life can flourish for long? On the other hand, this may be precisely what appeals to us in Rilke's writing when we feel indifferent ourselves to the needs of others or to our familial or social or political responsibilities in general. To guard against this sort of reading, it is sometimes necessary to sift the poems— including some very fine ones—with considerable care:

Abishag

Now David was old and stricken in years; and they covered him with clothes, but he begat no heat.
Wherefore his servants said unto him, Let there be sought for my lord the king a young virgin: and let her stand before the king, and let him cherish her, and let her lie in thy bosom, that my lord the king may get heat.
So they sought for a fair damsel, throughout all the coasts of Israel, and found Abishag a Shunnamite, and brought her to the king.
I Kings 1.1-3

I

She lay there. And her child-like arms were made
Secure by servants round the withering man—
On whom she sweetly lay as time dragged on.
He was so old she almost felt afraid.

And now and then she'd turn and push her face
Into his beard, whenever an owl hooted;
And all that Night was came, crowding the space
Which terror and desire had now transmuted.

The stars were trembling just as she was trembling.
Across the chamber wafted a curious scent.
The curtain moved by itself, like something resembling
Something in search of which her quiet look went.

But she held on tight as he grew darker, older;
And, out of reach of quintessential night,
She lay, feeling his kingly limbs grow colder,
A virgin and as light as a soul is light.

II

He sat enthroned and thought the whole dull day
Of things he'd done, of pleasure and frustration,
Indulging his favourite bitch's wish to play.—
But, in the evening now, Abishag swayed
And arched above him. His crazy life lay
Like a coast abandoned to its reputation
Beneath her silent breasts' curved constellation.

And sometimes, as the lover of many women,
He'd recognize through brows which needed trimming
Her unexcited, kissless mouth. He found
Her callow feelings' green divining rod
Was not to be tugged down to his deep ground.
He shuddered coldly; hearkened like a hound,
And sought himself in his last blood.

Well, yes, no doubt David *was* a great king and a great poet and here achieves, in Heidegger's famous phrase, "an impassioned FREEDOM TOWARDS DEATH". But what happened to the girl? And is her unexcited kisslessness under these circumstances really likely to have been a question of her *callowness?* Like other artists of the period, Rilke not infrequently underrated or discounted or, alternatively, idealized women in relationship to male energy or creativity (his poetry rather obviously suffers from his not having lived *with* a woman for any length of time) . . . And what, for that matter, about the rest of King David's dying? One has only to read on in *I Kings* 1–2 to encounter the gory details, the familial in-fighting and political power-play, surrounding the accession of Solomon, and the removal by assassination of his and his father's enemies. At times, one prefers the tough-minded worldliness of Heine, for example, as even the most devoted admirer of Wordsworth—equally high-minded and magnanimous, and another Romantic who transcended Romanticism—may sometimes prefer Byron:

King David

Now the days of David drew nigh that he should die; and he charged Solomon his son, saying, I go the way of all the earth: be thou strong, therefore, and shew thyself a man;
And keep the charge of the Lord thy God, to walk in his ways, to keep his statutes, and his commandments . . . :
That the Lord may continue his word which he spake concerning me, saying, If thy children take heed to their way, to walk before me in truth with all their heart and with all their soul, there shall not fail thee (said he) a man on the throne of Israel.
I Kings 2.1-4

> Smiling despots, passing on,
> Know their power is never gone:
> Though they die, it changes hands.
> Human bondage never ends.
>
> Poor plebeian nags and steers—
> Hauling carts for years and years!
> And the stubborn neck gets broken
> Which won't keep its proper yoke on.
>
> Solomon watched as David lay
> On his death-bed: "By the way,
> You had better keep an eye on
> General Joab, o my scion.
>
> "That old ruthless die-hard gets
> Generally on my tits.
> But he's weathered wars and purges,
> And I daren't indulge my urges.
>
> "You, my son, are wise and strong,
> Godly and, above all, young—

And you shouldn't have much trouble
Bursting Joab's hoary bubble."

A frequent and unashamed fibber in his life, Heine was incapable in his poetry of fudging a moral issue. What we would all love, I imagine, would be a poetry for our time as capable of ethical as of emotional and spiritual acumen. In the meantime, we had better be grateful for the poets we have. And if one were asked to choose? Well, if the ethical can—wittingly or unwittingly—help to conserve or even lead us to the waters of the spirit but can't make us drink them, the spiritual can baptize or subsume the ethical. And so it's clear which is—if not in fact, at least potentially—the more comprehensive:

"*O sage, Dichter, was du tust?*"

Say, poet what it is you do?—I praise.
But Death and nightmare mar our days:
How can you stand, how stomach them?—I praise.
But all that lacks a name, the Anonymous,
How, poet, can you summon it?—I praise.
Masked and disguised in ever-changing ways,
What right have you to claim the truth?—I praise.
And why should star and storm both recognize
In you their peace and strife?—Because I praise.

*

As a final exhibit, or translation/quotation, in this reconsideration (however incomplete) of Rilke's poetry, the reader might like to (re)consider, without further comment, the following short series of 'Seven Poems' which Rilke wrote in late 1915 while living in the Keferstrasse near the Englischer Garten in Munich, where his landlady was (as he expressed it in a letter) "a blonde and very beautiful and quite special woman who has rented me the 2nd floor while her husband is away". As far as I know, it is not known whether the poems were inspired by Rilke's landlady, or by the twenty-three-year-old painter Lulu Albert-Lasard, with whom he was having an affair at the time, or by no one in particular. At approximately the same time as he was writing the poems, heavy fighting was reported in France, the Balkans, Italy and elsewhere, so that he also found himself (as he also wrote) "a witness to the world's disgrace". The question therefore arises, as so often with Rilke, of whether the poems are a form of withdrawal or of spiritual progress:

SEVEN POEMS (1915)

i

The girl who gathers roses suddenly
Grasps the full bud of his life-giving limb
And, shocked by the difference of him/her, her/him,
Her [fragrant] gardens shrink, or try to flee

ii

The summer which, for me, you suddenly are
Has drawn the seed up into my soaring tree.
(Spacious within, o feel there the arching sky
Of Night, in which it stands mature!)
And now it rises into your firmament,
A growing image of real trees.
O fell him, so that (upside down) he sees,
Deep in your lap, the anti-Heaven meant
To make him really rear, really confront
Its dangerous landscape, such as prophetesses
Scan in their globes: that inner space
In which vast star-filled outer spaces hunt.

iii

Our glances close the circle, till a vision
Fuses the random tensions white in both
Of us—while your unknowing, blind decision
Raises a pillar in my undergrowth.

Stirred up by you, the god's tall image stands
At the silent crossroads, covered by my clothing;
My entire body invokes him. We are nothing
But spell-bound creatures on his spell-bound land.

And yet you must decide, if you're to be
Both grave and Heaven for the Herma. You
Can set the god amid his bee-swarms free
Of shrugged-off broken stone by letting go.

iv

Shy one, who know nothing yet of towers,
All of that's about to change
In the rich and strange
Space within you. Close your eyes, whose powers
Have, together with your face
And your innocent body, raised
One tower, rigid and complete. Amazed,
I inhabit towering space,
Into which I'm forced to cram
While you praise my progress—to the dome
Where across your soft night-sky I ram,
Like resplendent rockets shooting home,
Greater verve and feeling than I am.

v

How too much space dilutes us! till we're thin
As air, remembering superfluities.
And now our silent kisses sieve the lees,
Trickling with bitter wormwood or absinth.

How much we are! Out of my torso juts
A whole new tree, whose overflowing crown
Rises towards you. What would it be but
For the summer in your lap? Now fully grown,
Am I, are you, the one we satisfy?
And *who*'s to say as we both disappear?
A joyous pillar holds up the curved sky
Of our room, perhaps, and lingers longer here.

vi

To what are we closer? Death or the day
Of lives not lived yet? What would clay on clay
Be if the god were *not* to form the figure
Whose limbs now bud between us? But think bigger:
This is my body, which is resurrected.
Help him now quietly out of his hot grave
Into the Heaven which you and then I have,
Until our bold survival is projected
Through him—and you, young grove of deep Ascension.
You air of summer, dark and pollen-filled.
When all its thousand dancing spirits are spilled,
My stiff corpse gently sheds again its tension.

vii

How did I call you? With mute calls,
Which have become as sweet as they were wild.
As I push on inside you step by step,
My seed climbs on up like a happy child:
Ur-Mount of Venus, you, to whom we come, it
Breathlessly springs as I ascend your col.
Give in now—feel us coming—for you fall
The moment that we beckon from your summit.

after jandl

i

description of a life
(i.m. dietrich burkhard)

he has talent
the professor said to my mother.
he's very talented
my mother said to my father.
i have talent, the professor said to my mother
i said to my friend.

my father had a long life.
my father had hardly any white hair left.
my mother stopped plucking her white hair out hair by hair.
women don't want to develop a bald patch.
my father had so much time.
i won't be renewing
our acquaintance.

my name was dietrich.
at fifteen i wrote a tango.
i played the tango for my professor
and the professor said: i'll take care of
your further training and development,
and my mother said to my father
they'll take care of his training.

in 1926 i received my residence permit.
on it is written: 1926 to . . . .
19 in print and 26 in green ink
to the four printed dots;

the authorities were thinking of the third thousand years.
the authorities think a long time in advance.

my name was dietrich.
i had a talent for useless things.
in 1926 i received my residence permit.
i left primary school when i was nine.
at fifteen i wrote a tango.
at seventeen i passed my exams.
since 1944 i write the number 18
on official forms in the space for my age . . .

he has talent
the professor said to my mother.
he's very talented
my mother said to my father.
he should apply for something
my father said.
but i didn't apply for anything.

so they made me wear a grey jacket
and sat at home and wrote picture postcards
and cut their nails every day.
we'll take care of his training
the sergeant said to my mother,
and took the stalk of grass from between his teeth;
give that to his professor and tell him
it's not a question of talent, only of training.

my name was dietrich.
from 1926 to 1944.
now i don't have a name any longer.
from day to day there's less of me
and the enormous diggers of death
which for some time now

have quaked across the earth again
accelerate the process
of my further development.

    (*lebensbeschreibung* from *Dingfest*)

ii

what they can do to you

what they could do to you?
they could rip out your tongue.
you were never much of a speaker.
they could gouge out your eyes.
haven't you seen enough yet?
deprive you of your manhood.
you were never much use as a man.
dislocate your fingers.
you shouldn't pick your nose in any case.
hack off your feet.
at your age you ought to sit more.
torture you till you go mad.
everyone thinks you're crazy anyway.

    (*was sie dir tun können* from *Dingfest*)

iii

tell us about the war, dad
tell us how you signed on, dad
tell us how you shot 'em, dad
tell us how you were wounded, dad
tell us how you were killed, dad
tell us about the war, dad

(vater komm erzähl vom krieg from *Dingfest)*

iv

manner of speaking

i'll
break
you
yet
you
get

fatherbendmerather

(redensart from *Sprechblasen)*

v

cromwell

the horizon says goodnight
and chops off heads like trees
hardly have they said amen
before they're spiked on their dreams

mrs cromwell comes and crows till they wake
grafts each head to a neck
paints cuckold blood on the stitches
soon something stirs in the commonwealth

(cromwell from *Dingfest)*

vi

16 years

thickthdeen years
thentral thdayshun
thickthdeen years
what'th hegoin
what'th hegoin
to do
thentral thdayshun
thickthdeen years
what'th hegoin
what'th hegoin
the lad
what'th hegoin
to do

what'th hegoin
what'th hegoin
to do
thickthdeen years
thentral thdayshun
what'th hegoin
to do
the lad
with hith
thickthdeen years

    (16 jahr from *Laut und Luise)*

vii

she can cook

lots of dogs old women girlsheads and other needs or wishes
all get thrown into the one bucket
when she walks through the streets.
like a housewife home from market she empties on the
                                                        kitchen table
kraut radishes fruit and prawns out of her shoppingbag
rolls the old women lots of dogs and the girlsheads
like raisins nuts and lemonpeel
in the pastry of her needs
or wishes—opens herself and is the oven
which does the baking. she can cook.

    (sie kann kochen from *Dingfest)*

viii

in the deli

could you give me some maymeadow conserve, please,
fairly high up but not so steep
that you can't sit down on it.

well, then perhaps a snowy slope, deepfrozen,
containing no skiers, and a nice firtree
hung with snow, if you happen to have one.

then what about—hares, i see you've hung some hares.
two or three will do. and of course a hunter.
where do you hang your hunters?

(*im delikatessenladen* from *Dingfest*)

ix

surfacetranslation

*du bist wie eine blume
so hold und schön und rein
ich schau dich an und wehmut
schleicht mir ins herz hinein.*

*mir ist als ob ich die hände
aufs haupt dir legen sollt
betend dass gott dich erhalte
so rein und schön und holt.*

(heinrich heine)

do pissed v. iron a bloomer
so halt & sean & ryan
hicks how dick ann away mute
sh liked mere inns hurts he nine.

mere hissed al sob hick the end a
ow/eff sow/put deer lay gun salt
bait end ass got dicker halter
so ryan & sean & halt.

(oberflächenübersetzung from *Sprechblasen)*

x

antipodes

    a sheet
and under it
    a sheet
and under that
    a sheet
and under that
    a sheet
and under that
    a table
and under that
    a floor
and under that
    a room
and under that
    a cellar
and under that
    an earth

and under that
   a cellar
and under that
   a room
and under that
   a table
and under that
   a sheet
and under that
   a sheet
and under that
   a sheet
and under that
   a sheet

(*antipodes* from *Der künstliche Baum*)

xi

sonnet

an a an e an i an o a you
a you an a an e an i an o
a you an a an e an i an o
an a an e an i an o a you

an a an e an i an o a you
a you an a an e an i an o
a you an a an e an i an o
an a an e an i an o a you

an o a you an a an e an i
an i an o a you an a an e
an e an i an o a you an a

an o a you an a an e an i
an i an o a you an a an e
an e an i an o a you an a

   (sonett from *Der künstliche Baum)*

xii

wht y cn d wtht vwls

kss
fck
lck
sck
pss
sht

   (ohne vokale from *Der künstliche Baum)*

xiii

judgement

the poems of this man are useless.

to start with
i rubbed them into my bald patch.
to no effect. they failed to make my hair grow.

thereupon
i dabbed them on my spots. but these
grew as big as potatoes in only a day or two.
the doctors were astounded.

thereupon
i cooked a couple.
somewhat mistrustful, i refrained from eating them,
as a result of which my dog died.

thereupon
i used them as contraceptives
and paid for an abortion.

thereupon
i wore one as a monocle
and joined a better club.
the doorman
tripped me as i entered.

thereupon
i pronounced judgement as above.

(urteil from *Dingfest)*

xiv

perfection

e
ee
eei
eeio

p
pr
prf
prfc
prfct
prfctn

ep
eepr
eeiprf
eeioprfc
eeioprfct
eeioprfctn

pe
pree
prfeei
prfceeio
prfcteeio
prfctneeio

prfcteneio
prfcetneio
prfectneio
prefctneio
perfctneio

perfctenio
perfcetnio
perfectnio

perfectino
perfection

(perfektion from *Sprechblasen)*

xv

higher and higher

THE MAN CLIMBS ON THE CHAIR
the man stands on the chair
THE CHAIR CLIMBS ON THE TABLE
the man stands on the chair
the chair stands on the table
THE TABLE CLIMBS ON THE HOUSE
the man stands on the chair
the chair stands on the table
the table stands on the house
THE HOUSE CLIMBS ON THE MOUNTAIN
the man stands on the chair
the chair stands on the table
the table stands on the house
the house stands on the mountain
THE MOUNTAIN CLIMBS ON THE MOON
the man stands on the chair
the chair stands on the table
the table stands on the house
the house stands on the mountain
the mountain stands on the moon
THE MOON CLIMBS ON THE NIGHT
the man stands on the chair
the chair stands on the table
the table stands on the house
the house stands on the mountain
the mountain stands on the moon
the moon stands on the night

(immer höher from *Der künstliche Baum)*

xvi

time flies

fantastic!
fanfantastictic
fanfunfantastictoctic
funfanfunfantastictoctictoc
fanfunfanfunfantastictoctictoctic

(*die zeit vergeht* from *Sprechblasen*)

xvii

otto's mog

otto's mog flops
otto: on, mog, on
otto's mog hops off
otto: oho oho

otto totes coal
otto totes oats
otto stops
otto: mog mog
otto hopes

otto's mog knocks
otto: come, mog, come
otto's mog comes
otto's mog squats
otto: ogodogod

(*ottos mops* from *Der künstliche Baum*)

xviii

owls

you owls
yes
i'm owls

yes yes
very owls

you owls too
yes
i'm owls too
very owls
yes yes

but don't want to be owls any more
been owls too long already

yes
with you here
with you here too
i'm not owls any more
i'm not owls any more either
yes yes
yes yes too

but once you've been owls
you're always owls
yes

yes yes

(eulen from *Laut und Luise)*

xix

fifth now

door open
one out
one in
fourth now

door open
one out
one in
third now

door open
one out
one in
second now

door open
one out
one in
next now

door open
one out
you in
mornin'doctor

(*fünfte sein* from *Der künstliche Baum*)

xx

long load

some people think
that light and reft
can never be
contused.
        Tub bat's
a thig misfake!

    (lichtung from *Laut und Luise)*

xxi

two handsigns

i cross myself
before every church
i cherry myself
before every orchard

how i do the first
all catholics know
how i do the other
i alone

    (zweierlei handzeichen from *Laut und Luise)*

xxii

book and nose

it was a book, and again
a book, and another, and another one
and many others; he picked one up,
leafed quickly through it, and then another,
and another one, leafing
and finding nothing, nothing at all
for him.
nothing for him now, till he remembered
dietrich's nose, his blond head
and long thin fingers, which raised
the book, some book, open till it cracked,
to his nose, which then inhaled
its bookish fragrance deeply.
dietrich whose life, before the war
ended, had ended.

(buch und nase from *Der gelbe Hund)*

xxiii

fallen

he fell, and now
he fell too—he,
often enough, had fallen
on his knee, and scraped
the skin, so that his mother
treated it then
with iodine. But

he fell here sounds so
heavy as if more
must have happened than
a bleeding knee, a burn, a scab
and lastly some pink
now where the scab
has fallen off.

    (*gefallen* from *Der gelbe hund*)

xxiv

contents

i have nothing
to make a poem

a whole language
a whole life
a whole mind
a whole memory

i have nothing
to make a poem

    (*inhalt* from *Der gelbe hund*)

From SELF-PORTRAIT AS A WHITE COLLAR-WORKER (4)

i

Working for the Enemy

No work on "our side" meant that he—"like a spy"—
Felt forced to slave for umpteen years on "theirs":
For the sake of his art, he claimed—to leave it free
Of markets, fashions, cliques, to do or be
Whatever it needed. At last, the job and its cares
Silenced him. Left him puzzling over why.

He thought he'd grown, perhaps, to believe his lies:
At first we act them, then we act on them.
Once an escape from the gold-and-ivory tower,
"Useful experience" had gradually assumed more power
Over his heart and mind—by guilt and shame
As well as muddied, muddled compromise—

Than he'd ever expected. Though he held that art
Can swallow any subject—even the pride
Of the wounded artist—he knew as well that he ought
To have left that place where bodies and souls are bought,
Whose ways are all dead ends, where he might have died—
Of stomach cancer, say, or a stricken heart—

But, dully, suffered on. Self-punishment
Takes many forms. A more or less settled gloom
Grew slowly thicker, rarely now relieved
By doing things in which he still believed—
By looking forward to less fear, less boredom—
Or saying, for instance, what he really meant.

Disgusted, insecure, self-alienated,
Yet still condoning corporate power and greed,
He also told himself such sacrifice—
Which only went to show how little choice
We really have—was needed if the needs
Of his family were to be accommodated . . .

And so he managed. While others managed the world.
But art needs deep slow truth, the spiralling peace
Beyond all understanding. Not, of course,
As therapy, or some hermeneutic pause
In the race for gold. Or even here. But at least
As an end—in view or not—whereto we're swirled

Like eddies in a stream. We write to live;
He lived to try and find the time to write:
"What poets need above all things is luck!—
Plus native wit, perhaps, or witless pluck—
To help them through this fight that's not their fight,
This give-and-take that's only *take* not *give* . . ."

And yet, when he retired, he wished he'd done
Something to try and curb the booming harm
To human nature and/or the Nature we share—
Their actual earth and water, fire and air—
Instead of (in secret) sounding a quiet alarm
In ever fewer words. The enemy won.

ii

North of the Future

The Curse

"Enough! or Too much"—Blake

The apple grew like any other fruit
In that ecstatic garden. But they knew—
Or thought they knew—its knowledge was the root
Of greatness. Till in their growing minds it grew
Like nothing else. The snake's experiment
Was programmed to pollute the atmosphere:
The only knowledge gained was fear
Of losing. And in ways they'd never meant
They now seemed bound to suffer. Since their choice
Would only double-bind them if reversed,
They claimed God's blessing—who were clearly cursed—
And soldiered on, attempting to rejoice
In their achievements. And their fate was such
That their first were last and their last were at least
An unsatisfactory, discontented beast
Condemned, by wanting too much, to *want* too much.

*

An Ordinary Day

As if you dreamt you were lying
On a beach in the summer sun.
But abruptly started crying
For help as the tide came in.

As if your cries were silent:
How *could* anyone help?
Electric terror jangled
From your knees through your groin to your scalp.

And the ice-cold sea came crunching
Closer. Soon its grey waves
Would bundle and lock your body
Into an unmarked grave.

"Not fair! Why me?" you spluttered.
"I've always done my best
To write about what mattered;
I'm a cut above the rest . . ."

As if the salt and bitter
Water could really drown
Your spirit. As if its current
Could drag you down and down.

Until, in your dream, you were watching
Your burbling face turn blue;
Until, absurdly, you realized
That all you needed to do

Was stand and walk out of the water
To where the beach was dry.
Which you did—and awoke. To the quietness
Of an utterly ordinary day.

*

The Blessing
    (after Chuang Tzu)

"*Who knows that life and death, existence and annihilation are a single body? I will be his friend!*"
    —Chuang Tzu, Ch.6

i

The Chinese Masters Yü and Ssu
Agreed in their hearts with Li and Lai
That all a Master has to do
Is be content—to live, to die . . .

When Master Ssu's white horse ran off,
His neighbours blamed it on bad luck.
But the horse returned with three wild mares:
Ssu thought, "What's bad? What's good?"

While breaking in the mares, Li's son
Fell and injured his back.
But imperial army recruiters took
His neighbours' sons: "Good? Bad?"

Li's son lay helpless on his bed.
Enemy soldiers came
And burnt the village. Now Li wept,
Even *if* all luck is the same,

For his only son . . . "But who can own
The stars, which take and give?
Things merely happen. I alone
Must make them die or live.

"And man alone, of all that dies
Beneath the silent sun,
Is blessed with procreative eyes—
To make things, or undo what's done . . ."

ii

Suddenly master Yü fell ill.
His body, twisting in a knot,
Grew crippled. Unconcerned and still,
Yu smiled on this and smiled on that.

When Master Ssu inquired if he
Was content with crawling on the ground,
Yü wrote in the dust: "To let life be"—
And he laughed—"is Freeing-the-Bound."

The next to ail was Master Lai,
Writhing and wheezing at death's door.
His wife and children raised a cry.
But Lai praised *Less* like praising *More*.

When Master Li inquired if he
Was content to draw his final breath,
Lai smiled: "Life's not at fault. To free
The bound, I praise my death."

Then Ssu and Li burst into song:
Sick Yü and dying Lai were right,
Content with change in the changeless Night.
How could the Way itself be wrong?

Acknowledgements & Notes

Some of the poems and translations in this book first appeared in the following magazines: *Acumen, Agenda, The Amsterdam Review, Babel, HQ Magazine, The Interpreter's House, Metre, Modern Poetry in Translation, Oxford Poetry, Pennine Platform, Poetry Nottingham, Poetry Review, Poetry Wales, The Shop.*

p.9 ***The Dance of Death*** **(after *Todtentanz der Stadt Basel*)**: The Dance of Death, or *Danse macabre,* developed as a genre in various parts of Europe after the arrival of the Black Death from Asia in the mid-fourteenth century. Over the next hundred years or so the ravages of late medieval war also contributed to its grim imagery. Wall-paintings were often accompanied by verses, as in the city of Basel. Apart from their effective juxtaposition of two complementary quatrains, the Basel poems are mostly plain and often cumbersome and I have frequently elaborated on them. However, I have preserved the original order of the poems, replacing the Painter and the Painter's Wife with the Poet and the Poet's Wife. I have also excluded the Jew, Pagan and Paganess—which leaves perhaps only the Usurer as obviously *punished* by Death. Otherwise, the emphasis (as was common) is on the inevitability of Death's usually unexpected and mocking arrival. Ingmar Bergman's masterly extension of the genre, *The Seventh Seal* (1957), shows the Church's efforts to present death by plague as a punishment for one's sins—believed by some, but not by others—as well as the terrible arbitrariness of when and where death actually struck. Even so, there is a sense in which Bergman's characters create their own futures—and the innocent, for example, escape for a time . . .

p.27 "**. . . *how you take it!*"**: *The Tempest* II.i.77. *Pace* the Arden (1961) edition, which remarks, "The sense is not at all clear . . .", the meaning of Sebastian's comment on Gonzago's "widow Dido" *(viz.* "What if he had said 'widower Aeneas' too? Good Lord, how you take it!") is clearly enough related to one of the play's main themes: i.e. things depend on how you take them. Shakespeare's dramatic irony in putting these and other ironic remarks in the mouth of one the tempest's most helpless victims is complex but effective.

p.29 ***Boccaccio in Florence***: Although he was almost certainly born in Florence—in 1313—Boccaccio spent most of his youth in Naples, where, as a son of the general manager of one of the biggest Italian banking concerns, the Compagnia dei Bardi, he had access to the enlightened, early-Renaissance court of King Robert of Anjou. His father had him trained in banking and commerce and, when nothing came of that, in canon law. But Giovanni persisted in pursuing a life of letters and established an early reputation primarily as a poet of courtly love. By the 1340s the family was back in Florence, where the bank—of which his father was a director—had its headquarters. Tradition has it that Boccaccio was never as happy there, but though in later life he twice revisited Naples the experience was a disappointment. In 1348, according to the famous Introduction to *The Decameron*, he witnessed the Great Plague of Florence, in which between a third and half of the population died, including his father and step-mother. I have included some of the details of Boccaccio's account of the *'magna mortalitas'* or Black Death, as it came to be known, at the beginning of my adaptation, in 'The Dream', of *Decameron* II,v, where my idea was to show how *The Decameron* might have started but presumably didn't. Nevertheless, the book was certainly written between about 1348 and 1350.

p.30 **I'm illegitimate too**: In spite of a stubborn tradition that Boccaccio's mother was a Frenchwoman, even a king's daughter—and that his birthplace was Paris—nothing in fact is known of her. He himself, however, according to Vittore Branca, *Boccaccio—The Man and his Works* (1976), had at least five illegitimate children, and never married.

p.31 **My sweet, she whispered, etc.**: Cp. Shakespeare, *Venus and Adonis*, ll.229–234. Although Shakespeare, in his principal adaptation from Boccaccio, *All's Well That Ends Well*, infuses the typical moral concern of his mature writings into the rather loose amorality of *The Decameron* (somewhat as Lessing turned Melchizedek's shrewd escape in I,iii into Nathan's moral and spiritual conundrum in *Nathan the Wise*—see *From Now to Then*), it is tempting to imagine that Boccaccio's primarily sensuous and sometimes virtually innocent world-view at this stage exercised an influence over at least *Venus and Adonis* and possibly other early work such as *The Rape of Lucrece*, whether through Tudor translations or even the original Italian, and at any rate by way of Chaucer. Be this as it may, I have used the *Venus and Adonis* stanza for 'The Dream', as being evocative of this phase of Shakespeare's writing. Of course, innocence and amorality, when they grow up, are easily corrupted ("Lilies that fester . . .") or may simply turn nasty, which is at least one thematic development between earlier and later Chaucer, the English poet most profoundly influenced by Boccaccio . . . As for my own variations on these themes, G.H. McWilliam, Boccaccio's doughtiest translator so far, has remarked that Boccaccio (like Ovid) is one of those great sources whom "countless major and minor European writers have plundered for the raw material of their own artistic creations", and I make no apology for joining the crowd. For further notes on the making of stories from other people's stories, see below on p.44 ***Lucrece* came first, etc.**

p.36 ***The Convent Garden***: This poem is based on *Decameron* III,i, as though it were the story which Boccaccio heard *Filostrato*—whose name means 'vanquished by love'—narrate in the cathedral. Apart from the two young nuns seeming somewhat brazen as they plan to wake up the gardener (cp. p.38), there is not the slightest indication in Boccaccio's version of events that anyone is doing anything they shouldn't. Similarly, in his version of 'The Dream', there is no indication that the hero does anything morally more reprehensible than allow himself to be tricked . . . Although Boccaccio seems to have suffered some sort of conversion around the age of fifty, and in later life came increasingly under the influence of the rather strait-laced Petrarch, who encouraged him in the writing of humanistic treatises in Latin, his earlier work in the vernacular obviously took a very different view of social or Christian mores from that of either Petrarch himself (whose reputation as a moralist as well as a poet was already flourishing) or Dante, their common master. Dante, of course, was famous for idealizing his love of Beatrice (as Petrarch later idealized Laura) and for plunging Paolo and Francesca into the Second Circle of Hell for so slight a crime as adultery—not to mention Bruno Latini and the sodomites further down. In *The Decameron*, on the other hand, while there is certainly an official morality, which is all right in its way, anyone with any sense doesn't pay it too much attention. And so almost anything goes: adultery is implicitly recommended to anyone bored with their spouse, clerics would be fools if they didn't make the most of any opportunity which the Good Lord places in their path, and all kinds of sexual excess, oddity and perversion (as it used to be called) are taken for granted and enjoyed. Typically, an unsatisfactory husband *(The Decameron* is "no country for old men") will be outsmarted by a better man, and the wife and her lover will discreetly continue to enjoy their illicit love. Nor is there the slightest hint of irony when Boccaccio ends such stories, as he often does, with the likes of "May God grant that we enjoy ours also."

Apart from personal inclination, one possible reason for such changes in moral attitude between Dante (1265–1321) and Boccaccio (1313–1375) may well have been the appearance of the Black Death in Italy in 1347. Of the plague at this time and later, it has been said that only the most obstinately devout could have seen its unprecedented horror as part of some Dantesque or medieval divine plan. Philip Ziegler, in a long and complex chapter on 'The Effects on the Church and Man's Mind' in *The Black Death* (1969), considers the ways in which—although the plague did not directly *cause* the Peasants' Revolt or the Reformation—a state of mind had been brought into being in which doctrines were more easily doubted. He concludes by asking, "Does the statement that modern man was forged in the crucible of the Black Death have any real validity? Does it, indeed, mean anything at all?" As his whole chapter has shown, "In a field so amorphous any attempt at the precise or categoric would be futile. But if one were to seek to establish one generalization, one cliché perhaps, to catch the mood of Europeans in the second half of the fourteenth century, it would be that they were enduring a crisis of faith. Assumptions which had been taken for granted for centuries were now in question, the very framework of men's reasoning seemed to be breaking up." While Boccaccio does not go so far as directly to question the social or religious fabric of medieval society, he sometimes comes remarkably close to doing so, and an unmistakable atmosphere of *carpe diem* permeates the whole of *The Decameron*. At the end of his life Boccaccio returned to the Dantesque vision of things. But so, for that matter did Chaucer in his so-called *Retractions* at the end of *The Canterbury Tales*. In more recent times one need go no further than Tolstoy to find an author turning against his own earlier writings. And there are, of course, many parallel instances not only in the history of literature but of societies in general—as anyone who was young in 1968 and has survived into the age of Aids will be aware. It at any rate *matters* that we should try to distinguish such emotional swinging from side to side from genuine ethical or spiritual progress, even when these seem inseparable. Sadly, the twenty-first century's plague makes it as difficult to draw such crucial distinctions as it has ever been.

p.37 **God knows I've wept, etc.**: Cp. Chaucer, *The Merchant's Tale* (ll.1544–1553)—in which there is a more obviously post-lapsarian garden than in *Decameron* III.i. By his later *Canterbury Tales*, Chaucer had attained to a vision of humanity so clear and so tough-minded that if it had not been for his humour and compassion ("For pitee renneth soone in gentil herte"), it would be little less than terrifying. Chaucer was (self-)endowed with "a peculiar honesty, in a world too frightened to be honest", as Eliot wrote of Blake: "And this honesty never exists without great technical accomplishment" (*William Blake*, 1920). In his later tales, Chaucer's great gift lay in showing how people are and what they do, condemning no one and yet making his viewpoint perfectly clear. In this respect, his *Retractions* are more puzzling than Boccaccio's conversion, since Chaucer condoned nothing 'sinful'. In fact, the *Retractions* have been suspected of having been written under duress. Of which more elsewhere.

p.44 **Lucrece came first, etc.**: Cp. *The Rape of Lucrece*, ll.974–994. Shakespeare's other long poem is only superficially more morally aware than *Venus and Adonis*—its heroine kills herself not because she is so chaste that she cannot bear to live in this sinful world but out of physical shock or shame, wounded pride and a desire to avenge herself, however self-destructively, on her attacker. The behaviour of the (otherwise unnamed) Traversari girl in *Decameron* V,viii, on which *Nastragio* is based, is similarly self-destructive, and there was a close enough relationship, to my mind, between

The Rape of Lucrece and Boccaccio's story (Tarquin/Nastagio > the black knight; Lucrece/Traversari > the naked girl) to make the *Lucrece* stanza seem a natural choice for this adaptation. Moreover, Shakespeare almost certainly borrowed the stanza from its inventor, Chaucer, whose most famous poems in the form are *Troilus and Criseyde* and *The Clerk's Tale* of patient Griselda—both of whose sources, again, were stories by Boccaccio . . . Troilus himself is hardly more aware in Chaucer's poem than Lucrece (cp. *Troilus and Criseyde* Bk.V, ll.1219–1246, with **The next was *Troilus*, etc.** here). For Shakespeare, perhaps, Tarquin and Lucrece stood between Troilus and Criseyde to the one side and Griselda and her husband Walter to the other. In effect, the Necromancer (developed from *The Franklin's Tale*, itself a refinement of *Decameron* X,v) holds the mirror of art up to Nastagio's life by inviting him to consider these three archetypal relationships . . . In some respects, the "magicien" or "subtil clerk" of *The Franklin's Tale* resembles Prospero, as Shakespeare seems to have noticed:

> And whan this maister that this magyk wroughte,
> Saugh it was tyme, he clapte his handes two,
> And farewel! al oure revel was ago.
> And yet remoeved they nevere out of the hous,
> Whil they saugh al this sighte merveillous,
> But in his studie, ther as his bookes be,
> They seten stille . . .
> *The Franklin's Tale*, ll.1202–1208.

And so such stories continue to grow and, as it were, to annihilate time. Not, of course, that it is *necessary* to know their sources so as to read them. And yet one or another sort of re-creation, or necromancy, is clearly an age-old function of the poet's art. "For storytelling is always the art of repeating stories", as Walter Benjamin wrote, and "the more self-forgetful the listener is, the more deeply is what he listens to impressed on his memory . . ." Just as clearly, the notion that one should spin everything out of one's own entrails like a lonely spider is a relatively new or at least Romantic one.

p.46 **But next came that sweet peasant-girl, *Griselda***: Interestingly, Shakespeare's only mention of Griselda—in *The Taming of the Shrew*, II.i.288—is followed in the next line by Lucrece. Petruchio says of Katherina,

> For patience she will prove a second Grissel,
> And Roman Lucrece for her chastity,

providing a clear enough indication that the two archetypes were already associated in Shakespeare's mind. *The Taming of the Shrew* was written in about 1589 and *The Rape of Lucrece* was published in 1594—in 'rhyme royal', like Chaucer's tale of Griselda, as noted above. Shakespeare's own version of the Troilus and Cressida story came much later, of course, and is a very different kettle of fish . . . As regards the presence of Griselda and Lucrece in the taming of Petruchio's shrew as well as Nastagio's, my first reaction, on noticing the lines in Shakespeare's play, was to put this down to coincidence. Even so, Walter Benjamin's idea (in 'The Story-teller', 1936) of "the web which all stories form in the end: one ties on to the next" is profoundly attractive. And no doubt some knots lie deeper in Prospero's "dark backward and abysm of time" than we think.

p.49 **The Clouds dispell'd, etc.**: An adaptation of the end of Dryden's adaptation—entitled 'Theodore and Honoria'—of Boccaccio's story, in *Fables Ancient and Modern* (1699). Dryden was perhaps unhappy in love (the London of his time was in any case plagued by venereal disease), and his main addition to Boccaccio is an element of revenge in the behaviour of the black knight. However, in his versification and story-telling he is at the height of his powers. *Fables Ancient and Modern* (one of the glories of English poetry) also includes paraphrases from Chaucer. In his 'Preface' Dryden wrote: "So from *Chaucer* I was led to think on *Boccacce*, . . . the Genius of our Countrymen being rather to improve an Invention, than to invent themselves; . . . yet it appears that the Tales of *Boccacce* were not generally of his own making, but taken from Authors of former Ages, and by him only modell'd . . ."

As for the anachronisms here and elsewhere in *Boccaccio in Florence* (and anachronism in general), they are, I suppose, the now of Boccaccio's then, or the then of his now, or both. And a time-honoured now and then at that.

p.51 **The Chest**: This poem is an adaptation of *Decameron* VIII,viii and IV,ix, which present two different solutions to the problem of adultery, neither of which could be described as Christian.

Boccaccio's main interest in *The Decameron* was in a good story, and he was happy enough to approximate to one morality or another, depending presumably on his sources as well as his temperament. In the process, he sometimes illustrates unintentionally the common limitations if not glaring inadequacies of what we may like to think of as our ethics. Even on Day Ten, when he attempts (by way of an inspiring conclusion) to present ten stories about more virtuous people, his characters are for the most part more concerned with sexual or other politics (their reputations and social standing) than with genuine questions of good and evil . . .

p.54 **The sea, the sky, and Venus on a shell, etc.**: The description of the two sides of the chest is based partly on Chaucer's account of the temples of Venus and Mars in *The Knight's Tale*, ca. ll.1918–2050.

p.55 ***The fatal day, the appointed hour was come, etc.***: The italicized passage here is from Dryden's translation of Aeneas' description to Dido of the fall of Troy in *Aeneid* Bk.II.

p.61 ***His zealous men fulfil, etc.***: Adapted from the execution of Melanthius and the unfaithful servants in Pope's translation of *The Odyssey* Bk.XXII. The other italicized passages here are based on the end of Bk.XXI and beginning of Bk.XXII, in which Ulysses draws his bow and begins to slaughter the suitors.

p.67 ***The Gift:*** The epigraph is (mis)quoted from 'Ins and Outs', a section of *Colin and Colleen* in *From Now to Then* (p.219), and the poem relates to the Cromwell-motif which runs through that book. The final stanza is quoted as an 'old rhyme' by Christopher Hill in *God's Englishman*, and most of the details in the first seven stanzas are from Hill and Antonia Fraser, *Cromwell, Our Chief of Men*. The remainder of the poem has been assembled from various sources, such as Ovid, *The Tempest*, Coleridge, folk-tales, hagiographical motifs, etc.

p.71 ***Rainer Maria Rilke: A Post-Romantic Portrait (On Poetry and Death)***: The poems in this (re-)consideration or portrait of Rilke—executed partly in his own (translated) words—are taken mainly from the two volumes of *'Neue Gedichte' (New Poems)*, 1907–8. Rilke himself considered his *Duino Elegies* (1912–22), together with the *Sonnets to Orpheus* (1922), as the fulfilment of his lifetime's effort. The *Elegies* are written in a high-flown, hymnic style and in long, mainly dactylic but relatively free, unrhymed lines. However, some of his most condensed and powerful poetry is to be found in the more formal verse of *'Neue Gedichte'*. 'Turning Point' (xix) is a later work, and 'Sonnet to Orpheus' (xx) is the first section of the First Part of *'Die Sonette an Orpheus'*. Rilke composed his own epitaph (xxi)—about a year before he died in 1926 at the age of fifty-one. These three lines have multiple meanings and I have already translated/quoted them twice—at the end of *The Dance of Death* and at the beginning of *Words in the Dark* as the epigraph to *Then and Now* as a whole.

p.78 **An ancient, aristocratic ancestry**: Rilke's parents were, as he admitted in a letter, "in reality lower middle class", but "I had to wear very fancy clothes and until it was time for school went around dressed like a little girl". At the age of ten, when his parents separated, he was abruptly thrust into a military academy near Vienna. It has been said—and he implied as much himself—that he never fully recovered from the shock of being taken from his mother's over-protective arms to spend five spartan years training to become a professional soldier. Rilke was one of those writers—few in any age—who declare themselves to be nothing if not a poet, and single-mindedly live their lives accordingly. His poetry at its best is of great depth and intensity but may also be regarded as, among other things, a gut-reaction to the philistinism of his upbringing and as an attempt to transform or deny or even hide it. Josef Rilke (1838–1906), for example—the subject of 'Portrait of my Father as a Young Man'—was, in the words of Patrick Bridgwater *(Duino Elegies,* 1999) "a self-confessed washout, an army officer put out to grass as unpromotable, as unsuccessful in his life as in his marriage". Similarly, what his biographer, Wolfgang Leppmann politely refers to as "Rilke's conviction, avidly nourished for decades, that he was descended from an ancient and aristocratic family in Carinthia" had as good as no basis in reality: "As far back as it is possible to trace them, his ancestors had earned their living in the most ordinary of occupations, as farmers and estate managers, soldiers and officials. There is not a poet among them, not even a teacher, a scholar, or a clergyman." Of course, this kind of self-inflation is a common characteristic—one might almost say 'symptom'—of Romantic poets in general and is one good reason at least why we should treat their pronouncements—however beautifully expressed or otherwise meaningful or perceptive—with circumspection.

p.87 TRANSLATOR'S COMMENTARY: The poems by Rilke in this sequence are the first straight translations in the book, my aim being to get as close to the original in each case as was compatible with the attempt to produce a genuine poem in English. This is one of three sorts of translation in *Then and Now*. The others are the *re-make* (e.g. *The Dance of Death*) and the *adaptation,* as in the poems based on *The Decameron*. The difference between these is that the former takes a relatively unsophisticated or otherwise defective or only partially appropriate source and simply rewrites or 'borrows' from it, whereas the latter involves the calculated alteration or 'imitation' of an already sophisticated work of art so as to say something about it while producing a more or less autonomous text of one's own. Both re-makes and adaptations can just as well be of sources in one's own language: Shakespeare and Laurence Sterne provide examples of the former, and *Don Quixote* (which adapts the themes of Spanish romance) is an example of the latter, among other things. One tends to think of adaptation in this sense as a Modernist invention (Joyce's *Ulysses,* Picasso's many variations on other painters' pictures, Stravinsky's *Pulcinella* or *Cantata* or *Chorale Variations),* but art has always been made of other art as well as of life: Virgil would be unthinkable without Homer, Dante without Virgil. Interestingly, one does not need to know Cervantes' sources to see what he's up to, any more than one needs to have read Boccaccio's *Teseida* to get at least some of the point of Chaucer's *Knight's Tale*. Both re-makes and adaptations can validly make use of other people's translations, since they are likely to be some distance in any case from their original, and I have been grateful for the help of G.H. McWilliam with Boccaccio's Italian.

Of course, a map is not the territory, and most literary categories are no more than a rough guide. Even so, they have their uses. One reason why these particular distinctions, or something like them, are worth drawing is that the failure to do so can easily lead to the slippery slope of rewriting (i.e. treating as raw material for a re-make) the kind of highly wrought or densely considered text which demands as close a translation as possible because the more it is changed or interfered with the more it will be spoiled. This "crime of the mind", as Joseph Brodsky called it, tended in his experience to be less a question of incompetence or even indolence than of what he famously and persistently criticized (e.g. in three well-known pages on translations of Mandelstam in 'The Child of Civilization') as the excessive or immature "individuality" of translators: "Their conception of individuality simply precludes the possibility of sacrifice, which is the primary feature of mature individuality (and also the primary requirement of any—even a technical—translation)." Or ". . . all I want to do is prohibit something I haven't written", as he lamented elsewhere. Of course, a calculated adaptation is another matter, but the greater one's source the more essential it is that one should have something to *say* by changing it. Otherwise, one is in danger of committing an act of more or less gross disrespect—"at best a sacrilege", to quote Brodsky again, "at worst a mutilation or a murder".

p.88 . . . **a work made up entirely of quotations**: One of the main interests of *Then and Now* in translation has, of course, been as a form of quotation—if not to such an extreme as in Benjamin's claim. According to Hannah Arendt in her introduction to *Illuminations* (1968), Benjamin returns repeatedly to the theme of quotations in his voluminous writings. And one does not need to agree with his and Arendt's conviction that an irreparable break in tradition had occurred during the First World War and after to see what he means by the subversive and even destructive effect which quotations can have across the space between then and now: "Quotations in my work", he wrote, "are like robbers by the roadside who make an armed attack and relieve an idler of his convictions." On the other hand, quotations are only one aspect of the vast and complex landscape of intertextuality—as the great Modernists clearly realized—in which we may continue to reap and sow from then to now and from now to then.

p.89 **"Art can proceed from only a purely anonymous centre"**: Rilke had made similar observations much earlier than 1920. In 1912, for example, during a séance at Duino, he felt himself directed by an anonymous voice to Toledo, which was already associated in his mind with the mystical landscapes and angels of El Greco. In Toledo, Ronda, Córdoba and elsewhere, Rilke experienced not only in El Greco's paintings but in Spanish life what seemed to him to be manifestations of "truly everything which goes beyond the individual, in what direction I don't know, whether towards the future or towards the incomprehensible", as he wrote in a letter. Interestingly, another Spanish painter, Joan Miró, was already working his way towards a similar view of his art: "Great artistic periods", he wrote, "have always been dominated by anonymity. It is becoming more and more necessary today. At the same time, however, one also needs a totally individual gesture, one that is completely anarchic from a social point of view. Why? Because a deeply experienced individual gesture *is* anonymous, it opens the door to universality. I am convinced that the more limited something is the more universal it becomes . . ." Whatever one may think of "anarchic" here (subversive, certainly, of unthinking or rigid social mores), "a totally individual gesture"—like Brodsky's "mature individuality"—is accurately observed. And there are ways as well of producing at least an *effect* of anonymity, as a sort of post-Romantic antidote to Romantic egocentricity, including one's own—for example, translation. Others which may spring to mind re *Then and Now* are quotation, story-telling, and the many traditional metres and stanza-forms which "have been around longer than any poet . . . because they are themselves equivalents of certain mental states (which include ethical states)—or contain the possibility of curbing a certain state" (Brodsky, 'On *September 1, 1939* by W.H. Auden'). Even—or perhaps especially—that Romantic egocentric, W.B. Yeats, wrote towards the end of his life, in 'A General Introduction for my Work' (1937):

> If I wrote of personal love or sorrow in free verse, or in any rhythm that left it unchanged, amid all its accidence, I would be full of self-contempt because of my egotism and indiscretion, and foresee the boredom of my reader. I must choose a traditional stanza—even what I alter must

seem traditional . . . Talk to me of originality and I will turn on you with rage. I am a crowd, I am a lonely man, I am nothing. Ancient salt is best packing.

Nevertheless, free verse is, obviously, a valid and now venerable form in itself—i.e. an equivalent, in the context of Yeats's tradition, "of certain mental states (which include ethical states), etc.", as in xix and xxi here, *after jandl,* and many other sections of *Then and Now.* Of course, it is what we know of the tradition which gives all metrical forms their meaning, in the same way as all pronouncements, from individual words to poems and commentaries such as this one, derive their meaning from their context and mean more the more we know of it. In other words, if art proceeds (or should proceed) from the anonymous centre of an apparently headless Apollo, one might say that the *circumference* from which Rilke's god, in the beginning, drank in something which came streaming as if all song were entering him would now ideally be *panonymous:* "His head's too cool for bay-leaves, and the roses / Will *only later* grow as tall as trees // And form a garden, etc."

p.99 ***after jandl*:** Ernst Jandl (1925–2000) was a leading Viennese avant-garde poet and dramatist. In 1943 he was conscripted into the *Wehrmacht*. Taken prisoner by the Americans, he returned to Vienna in 1946, where he later taught English. *after jandl* is, like *Rainer Maria Rilke: A Post-Romantic Portrait,* an attempt to portray from a certain angle the original author of the poems which the sequence quotes, or, in this case, imitates. Since these were all written between 1952 and 1980, one might think of the sequence, in this respect, as a 'Post-*War* Portrait', and it is—or will be—part of a projected longer series involving German-speaking poets with direct experience of the Second World War, one of whose aims is to illustrate how they coped with what happened to them.

Like much of Jandl's writing (including his play, *Aus der Fremde*—see *From Hand to Mouth* in *Words in the Dark*), many of the poems which the sequence is based on were partly or entirely untranslatable—for example, that of ix *('oberflächen-übersetzung'),* which does the same sort of thing with Wordsworth's "My heart leaps up when I behold / A rainbow in the sky" as I have done with Heine's poem. Most of xx *('lichtung')* is, like ix, an 'imitation'. An earlier version of Jandl's famous word-play is to be found in *From Hand to Mouth*, xix. A few sections of *after jandl*, on the other hand, scarcely needed translating at all: in xii, I have merely extended the poem's idea to the title, the text being already in English; and in xiv, I had only to change one letter of the German *"perfektion"*. Lastly, xxiv is a version of p.5 of *Der gelbe Hund*, and not a misquotation of Jandl's own English on p.6.

p.118 **From *'Self-Portrait as a White-Collar Worker (4)'*:** Parts (1) and (2) of this sequence–within-the-sequence are to be found in *Words in the Dark* and part (3) in *From Now to Then*.

p.120 *"Enough! or Too much"*: *The Curse* virtually reverses the meaning of Blake's dictum in *The Marriage of Heaven and Hell*, where it implies that "The road of excess leads to the palace of wisdom"—a superficially exciting but half-baked idea, of the sort for which Eliot, after praising *Songs of Innocence and Experience* (see note on p.37 above), took him to task. The point of view of the poem is, rather, that of ecologists such as Gregory Bateson, who wrote in *Mind and Nature* (1979):

> Desired substances, things, patterns, or sequences of experience that are in some sense 'good' for the organism— items of diet, conditions of life, temperature, entertainment, sex, and so forth—are never such that more of the something is always better than less of the something . . . More calcium is not always better than less calcium. There is an optimum quantity of calcium that a given organism may need in its diet. Beyond this, calcium becomes toxic. Similarly, for oxygen that we breathe or foods or components of diet and probably all components of relationship, enough is better than a feast. We can even have too much psychotherapy [!] A relationship with no combat in it is dull, and a relationship with too much combat in it is toxic.

And so on. Bateson also observes: "This characteristic of biological value does not hold for money . . . More money is supposedly always better than less money." However, ". . .when we consider money, not by itself, but as acting on human beings who own it, we may find that money, too, becomes toxic beyond a certain point. In any case, the set of presuppositions by which money is supposedly better and better the more you have of it, is totally antibiological." Not to mention power—fame—technological prowess—and other idols of modern man. Eliot's response to the modern world was famously conservative:

> We have the same respect for Blake's philosophy . . . that we have for an ingenious piece of home-made furniture: we admire the man who has put it together out of the odds and ends about the house. England has produced a fair number of these resourceful Robinson Crusoes; but we are not really so remote from the Continent, or from our own past, as to be deprived of the advantages of culture if we wish them.

And yet "the divorce from Rome", which Eliot goes on eloquently to regret, was as inevitable as the collapse, in the meantime, of Protestantism (I exclude all forms of fundamentalism as irreligious). If not Robinson Crusoes, we are all Prodigal Sons and Daughters now, with no home to return to—as Eliot, in fact, was sufficiently aware: "The fault is perhaps not with Blake himself, but with the environment which failed to provide what such a poet"—and not just such a poet—"needed; perhaps the circumstances compelled him to fabricate . . ." What seems not to have occurred very clearly to either Eliot or Bateson is that a person or group of persons might free themselves sufficiently from "the circumstances" so as to be able to *choose*, not to "fabricate" (with its nuances of falsity), but to transform or re-create what they think and therefore do.

p.122 *The Blessing (after Chuang Tzu)*: As in *Lazarus* in *From Now to Then,* some of the ideas—and also certain phrases—in this poem derive from Burton Watson's translation of the Chinese Taoist philosopher, Chuang Tzu, especially Ch.6. The first section of the poem is based as well on a traditional Buddhist/Taoist parable, known to me orally.

www.ingramcontent.com/pod-product-compliance
Lightning Source LLC
Chambersburg PA
CBHW031151160426
43193CB00008B/331